Pretty Patchwork

by Leslie Linsley

Photographs by Jon Aron

Meredith® Press
New York, N.Y.

Dear Quilter,

Leslie Linsley has put together an unusual and delightful collection of innovative patchwork projects in this, her latest book, *Pretty Patchwork*. I know you'll enjoy selecting from this imaginative array of bright and colorfully designed patchwork, accessories, and quilts—both traditional and contemporary—offered in a wide variety of sizes and types, including standard bed quilts, crib quilts, wallhangings, pillows, curtains, tablerunners—even an assortment of fanciful sachets!

At Meredith Press, we strive to bring you the highest quality in quilting books. Each title comes complete with original designs and creative projects, easy-to-follow patterns and full-size templates. Instructions are clear and easy-to-read, and each project is accompanied by a full-color photograph for easy reference.

With *Pretty Patchwork*, you'll create beautiful patchwork and quilts that are enchanting, a pleasure to behold, and will surely add something special to your home or that of someone you love.

Sincerely yours,

MARYANNE BANNON
Executive Editor

Meredith® Press is an imprint of Meredith Books:
President, Book Group: Joseph J. Ward
Vice President, Editorial Director: Elizabeth P. Rice

For Meredith® Press:
Executive Editor: Maryanne Bannon
Associate Editor: Guido Anderau
Copyeditor: Sydne Matus
Proofreader: Robert Gillespie
Production Manager: Bill Rose
Design: Ulrich Ruchti

ISBN: 0-696-02389-X
Library of Congress Catalog Card: 93-077401

Printed in the United States of America
10 9 8 7 6 5 4 3 2 1

Contents

Introduction

Unless you've been living on Mars for the past ten years, you're well aware of the renewed interest in quilts and the popularity of quiltmaking. In the last decade there has been an overwhelming surge of interest in American folk art, but few items have become so popular as the patchwork quilt.

Quiltmaking has been part of America's way of life since our country was first settled. Patchwork, the sewing together of fabric to fabric to create a pieced whole cloth, is the only needlework that is truly indigenous to the United States. And although quilting was done worldwide, nowhere else did it become the art form it is in this country.

Quiltmaking was tremendously popular in the latter half of the 1800s, so a great number of antique quilts stem from that period, many of which have survived in good condition. These quilts are among the most prized collectibles because of their wonderful designs and exquisite needlework.

While antique quilts are appreciated for their historic significance, artful design, and skillful craftsmanship, the increasing interest in these quilts comes from a desire to recreate the old patterns with new materials. People who can sew are intrigued with the idea of making their own quilts and quilted projects, and this interest has opened up a whole new realm of creating for the home crafter. The projects are good-looking and useful, and, with leisure time at a premium, making quiltworks provides a most satisfying creative outlet. The results are also significant in that they help to carry on an American tradition.

Over the past ten years I've written several quilting books. In the beginning, the projects tended to be very simple and easy to construct. Most readers were timid about trying a new craft even though the technique of sewing wasn't new. Now, however, quilting is so pervasive in our society that quilters are anxious for projects that are challenging as well as those that can be done quickly in spare moments. Everyone seems to enjoy recreating the traditional patterns that have become so familiar from our country's past, but the availability of new fabrics adds exciting potential for reinterpreting the old to look more up-to-date.

Perhaps this is because quilted projects are a decorating mainstay. Quilts have become synonymous with country decorating. This style is no longer a fad. There is a vast movement back to basic, traditional comfort and quilts are part of this heritage.

Decorating our homes has become another creative pastime and Americans, as never before, have become design-savvy. Simply put, we like our homes to be aesthetically pleasing, reflecting an attitude that says we care about our living spaces. We all want pretty rooms. The decorating magazines show room after room filled with florals and prints used in every combination on beds, windows, tabletops, and furniture. Even if we can't afford to buy the products shown, the variety of fabrics available to the home sewer makes it possible to achieve a similar look.

Years ago, when quiltmaking originated, the fabric limitations determined the colors and prints used for quilting. Now, we have infinite choices and it's easy to create projects in any style imaginable. I love fabric shops. It's exciting to look at the possibilities for combining colors, prints, and textures. Most quiltmakers prefer 100 percent cotton fabrics, and fabric makers have responded with a wide variety of selections. I like pretty fabrics. I've been affected by the proliferation of floral prints, pastel stripes, overall geometrics that are more delicate than bold, and I especially like the array of shadings one finds for different colors.

The interest in decorating has influenced our choices of fabric for projects that will be used in a specific area of the home. For example, if we want to display a wall hanging in a room that has been decorated in floral chintz, we can make the wall hanging from the same fabrics used to slip-cover the sofa and find matching solids to create the patchwork design. It's also not impossible to find just the right fabric prints and colors for patchwork pillows to go with the rest of the decor. Making pretty patchwork opens up new design possibilities. For example, it's fun to see if the traditional Bear Claw or Churn Dash design, so familiar in solids and calicos can look just as good, if not better, when rendered with apricot and aqua floral prints (see page 95).

It's exciting to use new fabrics to create a traditional pattern. In a way, this is how we keep these Early American designs vibrant and give them new meaning within the context of decorating for modern living. The familiar feeling of country warmth is retained, but the old designs are refreshingly revived. I like the new fabrics and enjoyed working with them. The VIP, Concord, Peter Pan, and Waverly companies have extensive lines of fabrics designed especially for quilters. They look every bit as interesting as the more expensive fabrics made specifically for home decorating and they are 100 percent cotton. Fabric is the key to designing exciting projects and results are the proof. I hope you enjoy making the following projects as much as we did. Even if you can't find the exact fabrics we used, it won't be hard to find similar substitutes.

LESLIE LINSLEY

Getting Started in Quilting

QUILTING TERMS

Before starting any quilting projects it's a good idea to learn the basic terms of the craft. Quilting has been popular for such a long time that many different teachers have devised their own particular ways of doing things. Often a quilter who has had success with a pattern will be excited to repeat it with different fabrics. My mother made a Bow Tie quilt from scraps of fabric I had sent her. When she was finished she was eager to make another with an entirely different color combination. She had learned a lot from the first and was anxious to apply these skills to another project. This is the way shortcuts and new ways to do the same things over and over are devised and often passed along from one quilter to another.

Familiarize yourself with the basic terms before you begin so the directions for each project will be clearer. Knowing what's involved before you begin will help you decide which project you'd like to make. You can refer back to these definitions from time to time if needed.

Backing: This is the fabric used on the underside of the quilt. (See the fabric section (page 9) for types of material to use.) While I've given the exact measurement needed for the backing of each project, if you have extra backing fabric around the quilt top it should be trimmed after all quilting is complete, not before.

Basting: Long, loose stitches used to hold the top, batting, and backing together before quilting. These stitches are removed after each section is quilted.

Batting: The soft lining that makes the quilt puffy and gives it warmth. Batting comes in various thicknesses, each appropriate for different kinds of projects. Most quilts are made with a thin layer of Traditional Poly-Fil. Quilt batting is usually sold in pieces to fit different bed sizes. For this reason I've used the exact finished size of the quilt to give the dimensions of the batting needed for each project. In this way you can buy the package of batting closest to the size needed. However, when quilting it's always a good idea to have the batting be several inches wider and longer than the quilt top you are making. It will be trimmed after all quilting is completed.

Batting also comes in small, fluffy pieces that are used for stuffing projects, such as sachets, pincushions, pillows, and so on.

Binding: The way the raw edges of fabric are finished. Many quiltmakers cut the backing slightly larger than the top piece so they can bring the extra fabric forward to finish the edges. Contrasting fabric or bias binding is also used.

Block: Geometric or symmetrical pieces of fabric sewn together to create a design. The finished blocks are sewn together to create the finished quilt top. Individual blocks are often large enough to be used for a matching pillow. If you're a beginning quilter you might enjoy making a pillow as a first project.

Borders: Fabric strips that frame the pieced design. A border can be narrow or wide, and sometimes there is more than one border around a quilt. Borders often frame quilt blocks and are sometimes made from one of the fabrics or from a contrasting fabric. Borders are often used to enlarge a quilt top so that it extends over the sides of the mattress.

Traditionally, for the sake of interest, quilting patterns are stitched in the borders. However, many quilters leave this area free of stitches in order to complete the project in a shorter period of time. When borders are called for, these are usually the largest pieces of fabric to be cut and should be cut before the small patch pieces to be sure you have continuous strips. You want to avoid having to piece the border strips in order to make a nicer-looking quilt or wall hanging.

Lattice strips: The narrow pieces of fabric used to frame the individual blocks and join them together. They are often made in a contrasting color.

Mitered corners: Most borders butt at the corners, but a mitered corner is another option. This means that the ends of the borders are joined with a diagonal seam at a 45-degree angle. To do this, position one border over the other at one corner on the wrong side of the quilt. Draw a diagonal line from the outside corner to the inside corner where the borders meet. Reverse positions of the border strips (bottom strip now on top) and draw a line from the outside corner to the inside corner as you did before. With right sides facing, match the two pencil lines and stitch along this line. Cut away the excess triangular shapes and press seams to one side. Repeat on all 4 corners of the quilt.

Patchwork: Fabric pieces sewn together to create an entire design. Sometimes the shapes form a geometric block. The blocks are then sewn together to make up the completed quilt.

Piecing: Joining patchwork pieces together to form a design on the block.

Quilting: Stitching together 2 layers of fabric with a layer of batting between them.

Quilting patterns: The lines or markings on the fabric that make up the design. Small hand or machine stitches run along these lines, which might be straight, curved, or made up of elaborate curlicue patterns. Small quilting stitches can also follow the seam lines where pieces of fabric are joined. Or a quilting pattern can be created by stitching a grid of squares or diamonds over the entire fabric.

Top: The front layer of fabric with the right side showing. Patchwork or appliquéd pieces create the top fabric.

MATERIALS FOR QUILTING

Cutting board: This is a handy item for quick measuring and cutting methods you'll use for making quilts. It is available in fabric stores or from mail-order sources.

Fabric: You can never have too many different fabric patterns when designing a quilting project. I always seem to need ten times more variety from which to choose. Fabric is the main concern: what kind, how much to buy, and what colors or prints will work together.

Most quilters prefer 100 percent cotton and most fabric is 45 inches wide with selvage. All the fabric you choose for a quilting project should be of the same weight and should be washed before it is used. This removes any sizing in the fabric and allows for shrinkage. Sometimes cotton fabric fades slightly. This produces a worn, old look which is desirable in the world of quiltmaking.

When collecting a variety of fabric prints for your quilting projects, it's a good idea to have a selection of lights and darks. The colors and patterns of the fabric will greatly affect the design. Calico has always been used for quilting projects. The small, overall prints can be used effectively together, and there is a wide variety of colors to choose from. Pretty floral prints are lovely to use with alternating solid colors chosen to match the colors in the prints.

The backing fabric for a quilt can be a sheet, muslin, or one of the fabrics used for the patchwork on the top. It too should be 100 percent cotton, and generally a light color. A dark color might show through the thin batting and light fabric in the quilt top. Unlike 45-inch wide fabric, a sheet is wide enough to cover the back of any size quilt without piecing.

Iron: It's impossible to work on any project without having an iron right next to the sewing machine. After each stitching direction, you will be instructed to press the fabric. If you are doing patchwork, it's handy to pad a stool or chair with a piece of batting and place it next to you by the sewing machine. As you piece the fabric, you can iron the seams without getting up. Use a steam setting.

Marking pen: Sometimes a pattern or design has to be traced from the book and transferred to the fabric. When you want an overall quilting design, you'll need lines to follow. Water-soluble pens made specifically for marking your quilting lines can be found in fabric shops. Once you've finished quilting, the pen marks can be removed from the fabric with a plant mister or a damp sponge. Simply pat over the lines and they disappear.

Colored chalk pencils are used for marking quilting patterns on dark fabric. They come in all colors including white, and when the quilting is complete the chalk is easily brushed away.

Needles: All the projects in this book are pieced on a sewing machine. The quilting can be done either by hand or on the machine, but hand-quilting looks best. If the batting is extra-loft weight, it will not go through the machine and the quilting must be done by hand. Many quilters use this thick batting for tied quilts. However, most quilts are made with a Traditional batting. To quilt you'll need #7 and #8 sharps, which are the most common size needles used for hand-quilting. They are often called "betweens."

Rotary cutter: This tool looks like a pizza cutter and allows you to cut several layers of fabric at once. It is more accurate than scissors.

Ruler and yardstick: You can't work without them. A metal ruler can be used as a straightedge for the most accurate cutting. Use the yardstick for cutting lengths of fabric when you must mark and cut at least 36 inches at one time.

The width of the yardstick is perfect for marking a grid pattern for quilting. You simply draw the first line, then flip the yardstick over and continue to mark lines without ever removing the yardstick from the fabric. You will have a perfect 1-inch grid.

Scissors: You'll need good scissors for cutting your fabric. Try not to use these scissors to cut anything but fabric to keep them at their best. Cutting paper with scissors will ruin them. Invest in a pair of small, pointed scissors for snipping threads as you stitch and quilt.

Stencil: Many quilt patterns are available on precut stencil paper. This makes it easier to plan and transfer the designs to the fabric. You position the stencil on the fabric and mark through the cut lines onto the fabric. Some quilters like making their own stencils, and the materials are available in art supply and hobby shops.

Straight pins: Use extra-long 1¾-inch sharp pins.

Template: A rigid, full-size pattern that is used to trace design elements. It can be cut from cardboard, manila, oaktag used for filing folders, plastic, acetate, or sandpaper. Acetate, which is transparent and produces clean, crisp edges, should be used for pattern pieces when a repeat design is required. Sandpaper doesn't slip when placed facedown on the fabric. If you're cutting one design, simply use the paper pattern pinned to the fabric as a cutting guide.

Thimble: I can't work with one, but I try from time to time because my fingers get numb from pricking them so often. Try one for hand-quilting but be sure to get the right size. I must admit, without it I run the risk of bleeding on my fabric.

Thread: Match the thread to the color of the fabric. Cotton-blend thread is best for all quilting and piecing.

QUILTING TECHNIQUES

Estimating Fabric Yardage

The fabric used for all of these projects is 45 inches wide. All measurements are figured with a ¼-inch seam allowance unless otherwise specified.

Every project lists the exact amount of material needed for each color, and all the quilt projects are made to fit standard bed sizes. Finished dimensions are given with each project. However, you may want to be sure that a particular quilt will fit your bed size, or you might want to change the size specified to something larger or smaller. It's easy to figure what size will best fit your bed.

When estimating yardage for a bed quilt, measure your bed fully made. This means with bed pad, sheets, and blankets over the mattress. Measure the length, width, and depth, including the box spring. Decide if you want a slight overhang, an overhang to the top of a dust ruffle, or a drop to the floor, and whether or not the quilt will extend up and over the pillows. If a quilt size for any project isn't the right size for your bed, it can be changed by adding to or subtracting from the border measurements. This shouldn't change the basic design.

Piecing the Backing

You may have to piece panels together for the back of a quilt, tablecloth, or wall hanging in order to get the correct size. Use the full width of fabric (usually 45 inches) cut to the appropriate length. Cut another piece the same size. To avoid a seam in the center of the fabric, cut the second strip of fabric in half lengthwise so that you have 2 narrow strips of the same size. Join one of these 2 matching panels to each long-sided edge of the large center panel. Press seams open. If you use a bed sheet the same size as the quilt top you will have a solid backing that doesn't require piecing. For some projects, a center seam on the backing isn't a problem since it isn't seen. This is especially true when making a wall hanging. The piecing of the backing fabric is a matter of preference.

Enlarging Designs

Most patterns and designs are shown full size, but sometimes they are too large to fit on a page. In this case, the designs are shown on a grid for easy enlargement. Each square on the grid represents 1 inch. This means that you will transfer or copy the design onto graph paper marked with 1-inch squares. Begin by counting the number of squares on the pattern in the book. Number them horizontally and again vertically. Count the number of squares on your larger graph and number them in the same way. Copy the design onto your grid one square at a time.

Transferring a Large Design

Trace the pattern pieces or quilting design from the book. Place a piece of dressmaker's carbon paper on the right side of the fabric with the carbon side down and the tracing paper on top. Go over all pattern lines with a tracing wheel or a ballpoint pen to transfer the design. Remove the carbon and the tracing paper.

Making a Template

If you use oaktag or cardboard for your template material you'll have to transfer the pattern to the template material by first tracing the design. Place the tracing facedown on the cardboard and rub over each traced line with a pen or a pencil. The outline will be transferred to the cardboard. Remove the tracing and go over the lines with a ballpoint pen to make them clearer. Cut out the design outline from the cardboard. If you use acetate, simply place it over the tracing and cut out the exact shape.

There are several advantages to using acetate for your template material. It can be used many times without losing its sharp edges and since it's clear you can trace a pattern piece directly onto it. Further, you can see through it when placing it on your fabric in order to position it where you want it. In this way, if you are using a floral print, for example, you might want to center a flower in the middle of the template piece. Draw a line from point to point on your template to make positioning it more accurate.

Determine which fabric will be used for each template. All the templates in this book include ¼-inch seam allowance, but you may even want to allow for ⅜-inch seams for easy turning of the edges. If the fabric is thick or the template design has points or curves it will be easier to turn the edges over if you have more seam allowance to work

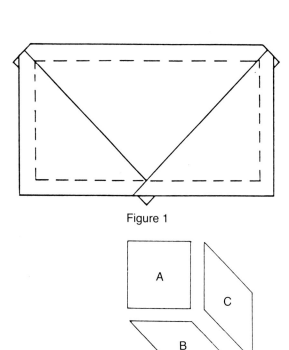

Figure 1

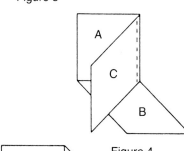

Figure 2

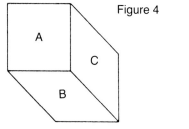

Figure 3

Figure 4

Figure 5

with. Try both space allowances to see which works best for you.

Consider the grain of the fabric and the direction of the print when placing your templates.

Sewing Points

Many traditional quilt patterns are created from triangles, diamonds, and similar shapes. The points present a challenge and require special care.

When stitching 2 such pieces together, sew along the stitch line, but do not sew into the seam allowance at each point (see Figure 1). It helps to mark the finished points with pins so that you can begin and end your seams at these marks.

Sewing Curves

Before turning a curved appliqué piece, stay-stitch (loose stitches) along the seam line, then clip or notch evenly spaced cuts along the edge in the seam allowance. Clip all inward curves and notch all outward curves. When the fabric is turned under, it will lie flat.

Sewing Inside Corner Edges

Place a pin across the point of the stitches and clip up to the stitches in the seam allowance in order to turn the fabric under.

Sewing Outside Corner Edges

Once you've stitched around a corner, clip off half the seam allowance across the point. Turn fabric back, press seams open, and trim excess fabric away.

Turning Corners

It's often a bit difficult to turn corners and continue a seam line. Figure 2 shows the 3 pieces to be joined. With right sides facing, stitch piece A to piece B as shown in Figure 3. Next, join C to A, as shown in Figure 4. Leave the needle down in the fabric. Lift the presser foot and clip the seam to the needle. Slide B under C and adjust so the edges of B align with C. Lower the presser foot and stitch along the seam line (see Figure 5).

QUILTING

Quilting is sewing layers of fabric and batting together to produce a padded fabric held together by small, straight, even stitches. The quilting process, generally the finishing step in a patchwork project, is what makes the project interesting and gives it a textured look.

Basting

Before quilting, you will have to baste the quilt top, batting, and backing together. To avoid a lump of filler at any point, begin at the center of the top and baste outward with long, loose stitches to create a sunburst pattern. There should be about 6 inches between the basted lines at the edges of the quilt. Baste from the top only. These stitches will be cut away as you do your quilting.

Hand-quilting

Thread your needle with a length of approximately 18–20 inches and make a small knot with a 1-inch tail beyond it. Bring the needle up through the back to the front of the quilt top where the first line of quilting will begin and give the knotted end a good tug to pull it through the backing fabric into the batting. Take small running stitches. Follow your premarked quilting pattern or stitch ¼ inch on each side of all seam lines. Do not stitch into the ¼-inch seam allowance around the outside edge of the quilt.

Machine-quilting

This quicker way to create a quilted look does not have the same rich look of authentic early quilting that hand-stitching does. It is best to machine-quilt when the batting isn't too thick.

When machine-quilting, set the thread tension approximately 6 stitches to the inch so the stitching looks like hand-stitching. Taking this precaution will assure that the absence of hand-stitching doesn't detract from the appearance.

Outlining

This is the method of quilting along the patchwork seams. In this way, each design element is pronounced and the fabric layers are secured(see Figure 6).

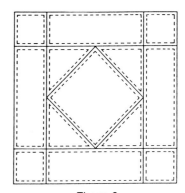

Figure 6

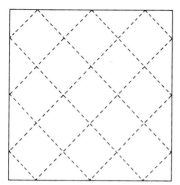

Figure 7

Overall quilting

When you want to fill large areas of the background with quilting, choose a simple design. The background quilting should not interfere with the patchwork or appliqué elements (see Figure 7).

To ensure accurate spacing, make grid patterns of squares or diamond shapes with a yardstick or masking tape. For a quick-and-easy method, lay a yardstick diagonally across the fabric and mark the material with a marking pen. Without removing the yardstick turn it over and mark along the edge once again. Continue across the fabric to the opposite edge. You will have perfect 1-inch spaces between each line. Lay the yardstick across the fabric at the corner opposite where you began and repeat the process to create a 1-inch grid across the top of the fabric. Stitch along these lines.

Tie-quilting

An alternative to hand-quilting is tying the backing, batting, and quilt top together at evenly spaced intervals in the center of blocks and the corners where blocks intersect. This is usually done with embroidery floss in the following way: Thread the needle with a length of floss approximately 10–12 inches, but do not knot the end. Insert the needle down through the top of the quilt through all 3 layers and back up again close to where you inserted the needle. Tie the floss in a knot and cut the ends to approximately 1½ inches.

QUICK-AND-EASY METHODS

Strip-piecing

This is the method by which you sew strips of different fabrics together and cut them into units that are arranged to make up the entire quilt top. This method is especially helpful when the project requires the piecing together of small or narrow pieces of fabric of the same size. Rather than cutting and sewing individual squares together over and over again, 2 or more strips of fabric are sewn together and then cut into segments that are exactly the same dimensions. These units are then arranged and stitched together in different positions to form the quilt pattern.

Right triangles

This is a quick-and-easy way to make perfect pieced triangles to create squares of any size. You can mark and stitch right-angle triangles before cutting. This is usually done when you want to create a square made of light and dark triangles or triangles of contrasting fabrics.

1. Begin by figuring out the number of pieced squares you'll need for the project. You will create a grid of squares on the wrong side of a piece of fabric, usually the lighter color, as shown in Figure 8. The number of squares will be half the number of squares needed for the project because you'll get 2 triangle pairs from each square on the grid.

2. Determine the size of your finished square and add ⅞ inch to it. For example, if you want to create 2-inch squares, mark off a grid of 2⅞-inch squares on the wrong side of the light fabric. It's a good idea to draw a few extra squares in case you make an error in stitching.

3. Next, draw diagonal lines through each square as shown in Figure 9. With right sides facing and raw edges aligned, pin the marked light fabric to the same-size dark fabric. Stitch a ¼-inch seam on each side of the drawn diagonal lines as shown.

4. Cut on all solid lines to get the individual squares made of light and dark or contrasting fabric triangles. You'll have 2 triangles in each square. Press seams to the dark side.

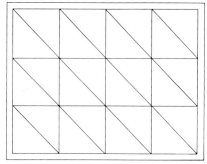

Figure 8

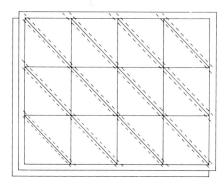

Figure 9

Binding a quilt

When a quilt is finished, the edges are bound in place with a narrow border of binding all around. Some quilters like to use the backing to bind the edges and often choose one of the fabrics from the pieced top for this purpose. To create a binding and narrow border all around the quilt you must cut the backing piece at least 1 inch larger than the finished top all around. Once the quilting is complete, turn the raw edges of the backing forward ¼ inch and press. Then turn this fabric forward to cover the raw edges of the quilt top and press. Pin in place, folding the corners neatly, and hand- or machine-stitch all around.

Purchased binding is made from bias strips of fabric sewn together. You will find packages in a variety of colors sold in most fabric shops. Several seams will be seen at various intervals along the binding but this is acceptable. It's not always easy to match the color exactly to those in your fabrics. Some quilters make their own bias binding by cutting strips of fabric (on the bias) to match one of the fabrics in the quilt top and stitching them together to create the length of binding needed.

Sewing small pieces together the easy way

When making a patchwork fabric from small (approximately 1½ inches) squares, there's an easy method for stitching them together. With right sides facing, pin individual sets of 2 squares each together. Stitch along one side edge but do not cut the thread when you reach the end. Simply run the machine for 2 or 3 more stitches and then feed the next set of squares through. Continue to stitch all the sets of squares in this way so you have a string of patches connected by the threads between. When you have enough for the project, cut the strings between the squares to separate them. Open each set of squares and press.

Hanging a quilt

Only quilts that are in good condition and not too heavy should be hung. There are three reliable methods for hanging a quilt or wall hanging. I prefer using a Velcro strip, which is effective if the quilt or wall hanging is lightweight and not too large. For this method, machine-stitch the non-gripping side of the Velcro to a strip of cotton tape, which is then hand sewn to the back top edge of the quilt. Stitch the tape to the backing fabric and batting only, not through to the quilt top, and stop short of each end. The gripping side of the Velcro is then glued to a length of lath (available in lumber yards) slightly shorter than the width of the quilt. Nail the lath to the wall and then attach the quilt to the lath. You may want to attach the bottom of the quilt in the same way.

Another method is preferable for heavier quilts. Make a fabric sleeve approximately 3½–4 inches deep and an inch shorter than the quilt on each end. Hand sew it to the back of the top edge of the quilt, again stitching through the backing and batting but not to the quilted top side. Insert a thin piece of wood, curtain rod, or dowel through the sleeve and suspend it at each end on brackets or other hangers.

An alternative for light quilts and wall hangings is to use Velcro to attach them to a set of artist's stretcher bars for hanging. These are available in various sizes in art supply stores.

SEWING TIPS

1. To continue hand-quilting without interruption, thread several needles at a time and weave them through a place mat. When you run out of thread from one needle, switch to the next. When not in use, the place mat can be rolled up easily for storage in a drawer with other supplies.

2. To stitch a perfectly straight line, stick a piece of masking tape on the fabric and stitch alongside the edge.

3. To keep fabric clean and visible, store it in clear plastic sweater boxes.

4. To pick up spilled pins quickly, place a nylon stocking over the vacuum suction nozzle and go over the floor. Hold the nozzle over the pin box, turn off the vacuum, and the pins will fall into the box.

5. To thread a needle with ease, stiffen the end of the thread with clear nail polish.

6. The acetate lids of stationery boxes are excellent for making patchwork and appliqué templates. You can see through them to trace a design right on the plastic and the edges will stay sharp through many uses. Further, you can position them on the fabric just where you want them.

7. Cut pattern pieces from wax-coated freezer paper and place them facedown on the back of your fabric. Pressing lightly with a warm iron will make the paper adhere so you can cut the pieces without using pins or basting.

8. To remove pencil marks from quilts, use an art-gum eraser.

9. When cutting pieces for making a quilt, it's always best to cut the border strips first, then fit the other pieces on the remaining fabric. In this way the border for each side will be cut as one continuous strip and you won't have to piece it.

10. Always wash new fabric before cutting and piecing. Fabrics shrink differently and some colors bleed when washed. It's better to find out before you wash a newly made quilt for the first time.

Pastel Baskets

Maggie Detmer made this quilt for her bedroom in her house on Nantucket Island. She favors the use of solid pastel colors for most of her designs. The finished quilt measures 73 × 87 inches, which is perfect for a double or queen-size bed.

MATERIALS

Note: Yardages are figured for fabric 45 inches wide.

¼ yard each of 3 different dark color solid fabrics
¼ yard each of 5 different medium color solid fabrics
¼ yard each of 3 different light color solid fabrics
½ yard each of 3 different paler color solid fabrics
½ yard tan solid fabric
½ yard light rose solid fabric
½ yard gray solid fabric
¾ yard pink solid fabric
2¼ yards black solid fabric (borders)
4¼ yards dark rose solid fabric (backing)
quilt batting 73 × 87 inches
tracing paper
cardboard
quilt marking pen and light chalk pencil (for marking black fabric)

CUTTING LIST

Note: All measurements include a ¼-inch seam allowance.
Trace patterns A, B, C, D, and E and transfer them to cardboard for templates (see page 13).

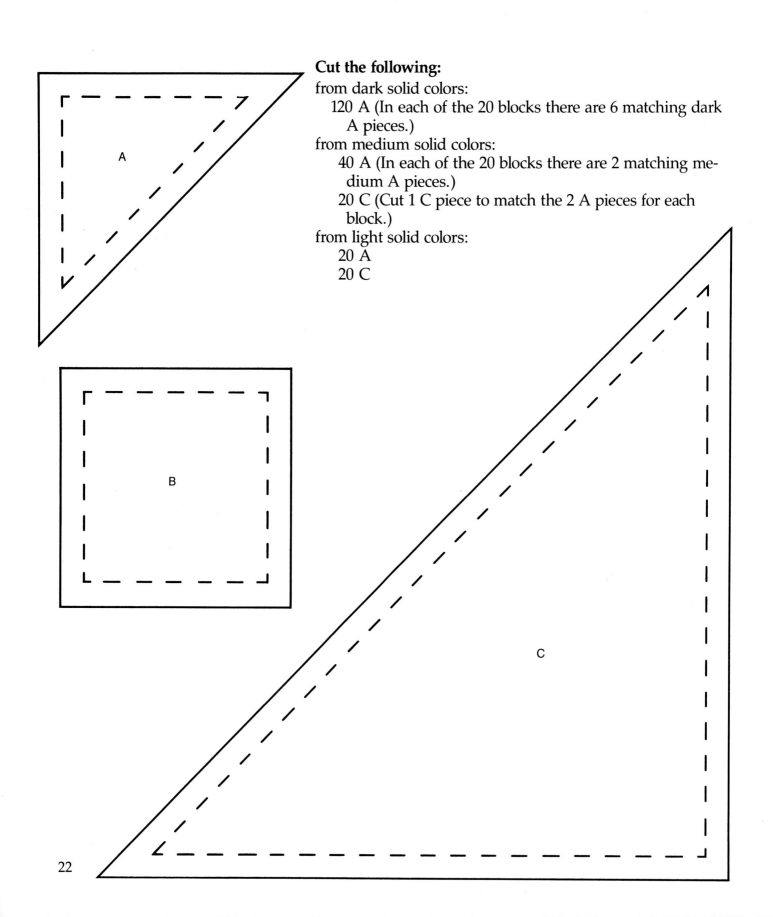

Cut the following:

from dark solid colors:

120 A (In each of the 20 blocks there are 6 matching dark A pieces.)

from medium solid colors:

40 A (In each of the 20 blocks there are 2 matching medium A pieces.)

20 C (Cut 1 C piece to match the 2 A pieces for each block.)

from light solid colors:

20 A

20 C

A

B

C

22

from pale solid colors:

   120 A (In each of the 20 blocks there are 6 matching A pieces.)

   20 B (Cut 1 B piece to match the 6 A pieces for each block.)

   40 D (Cut 2 pieces for each block in a different color from A and B pieces.)

   20 E (Cut 1 piece in each block to match D pieces.)

from tan solid:

   4 squares, each $10\frac{1}{2} \times 10\frac{1}{2}$ inches

from light rose solid:

   4 squares, each $10\frac{1}{2} \times 10\frac{1}{2}$ inches

from gray solid:

   4 squares, each $10\frac{1}{2} \times 10\frac{1}{2}$ inches

from pink solid:

   7 squares, each $10\frac{7}{8} \times 10\frac{7}{8}$ inches (Cut each square along the diagonal to make 2 triangles each, for a total of 14 triangles.)

   1 square, $11\frac{1}{4} \times 11\frac{1}{4}$ inches (Cut each square along the diagonal in both directions to make 4 triangles.)

from black solid:

   2 strips, each $8\frac{1}{2} \times 72\frac{1}{2}$ inches (top and bottom borders)

   2 strips, each $8\frac{1}{2} \times 70\frac{1}{2}$ inches (side borders)

D

E

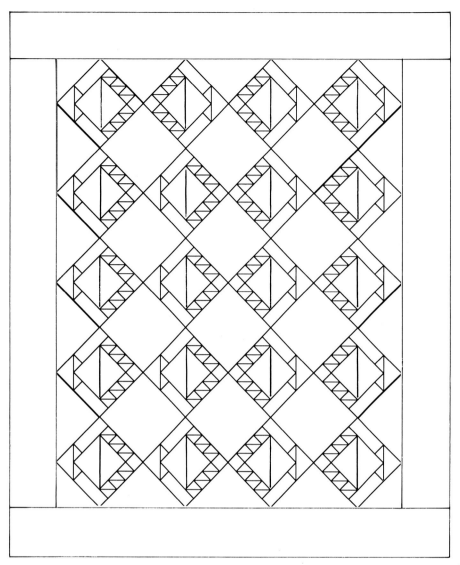

Figure 8

To join borders

Refer to Figure 8.

1. With right sides facing, join a shorter black border strip to one side edge of the quilt top.

2. Press seams to one side.

3. Repeat on the opposite side edge.

4. Join the remaining black border strips to the top and bottom edges of the quilt top.

5. Press seams to one side.

To prepare backing

See page 12 to stitch backing without a center seam.
1. Cut the backing fabric in half crosswise to make 2 pieces, each 45 × 76 inches.
2. With right sides facing, join along one side edge to make a piece 76 × 89½ inches.
3. Press seams to one side.

To transfer quilt patterns

Refer to page 13 for instructions for tracing and transferring patterns.
1. Trace the Quilting Patterns 1, 2, and 3. Pattern 1 represents one-quarter of the full pattern to be transferred to the 2 center solid blocks. Position Pattern 1 on each center block, and transfer; repeat 3 more times rotating to complete the circle.

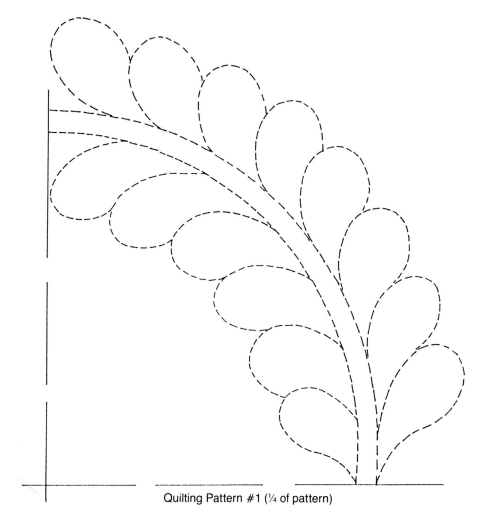

Quilting Pattern #1 (¼ of pattern)

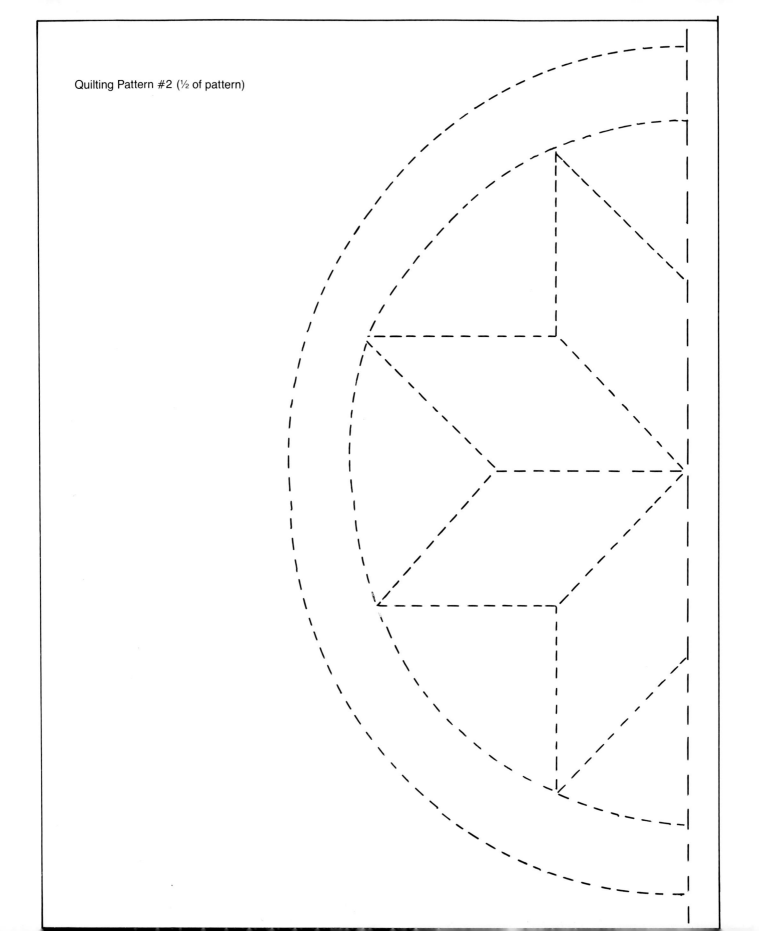

Quilting Pattern #2 (½ of pattern)

2. Pattern 2 represents one-half the full pattern to be transferred to the remaining solid blocks. To do this, position the pattern on the block, transfer it and then turn the pattern over and transfer it again to complete the star pattern.

3. Transfer Pattern 2 to the large pink triangles and one-half of Pattern 2 to the 4 small pink triangles.

4. Transfer Pattern 3 to the borders.

To quilt

1. With wrong sides facing and batting between, pin the backing, batting, and top of quilt together.

2. Beginning at the center and working outward in a sunburst pattern, take long, loose basting stitches through all 3 layers, stopping short of the seam allowance all around the outside edges.

3. Using small running stitches, quilt on all premarked lines and ¼ inch on each side of all seam lines.

To finish

1. When all quilting is complete, remove the basting stitches.

2. Trim the batting ¼ inch smaller than the quilt top all around.

3. Trim the backing so it's 1 inch larger than the quilt top all around.

4. Fold the backing edges forward ¼ inch and press. Then bring the remaining fabric forward over the top of the quilt to form a ½-inch border all around. Press and pin.

5. Slip-stitch the border to the quilt top to finish.

Pineapple Throw

Kate McCombe chose deep shades of warm colors to make this quilt with a wintry feeling. Although made up of sixteen identical blocks, the assembled pattern is quite interesting. The finished size is 53 × 53 inches and the quilt can be used as a wall hanging or a lap throw.

MATERIALS

Note: Yardages are figured for fabric 45 inches wide.
½ yard tan calico
2 yards rust calico
2 yards green calico
3 yards floral print fabric
3½ yards brown calico (includes backing)
quilt batting 53 × 53 inches
1 skein tan embroidery floss for tying
tracing paper
cardboard

CUTTING LIST

Note: All measurements include a ¼-inch seam allowance. Trace patterns A, B, C, D, E, F, G, H, I, and J and transfer them to cardboard for templates (see page 13).

Cut the following:
from tan calico:
　64 J
from rust calico:
　2 strips, each 1 × 44½ inches (top and bottom borders)
　2 strips, each 1 × 45½ inches (side borders)

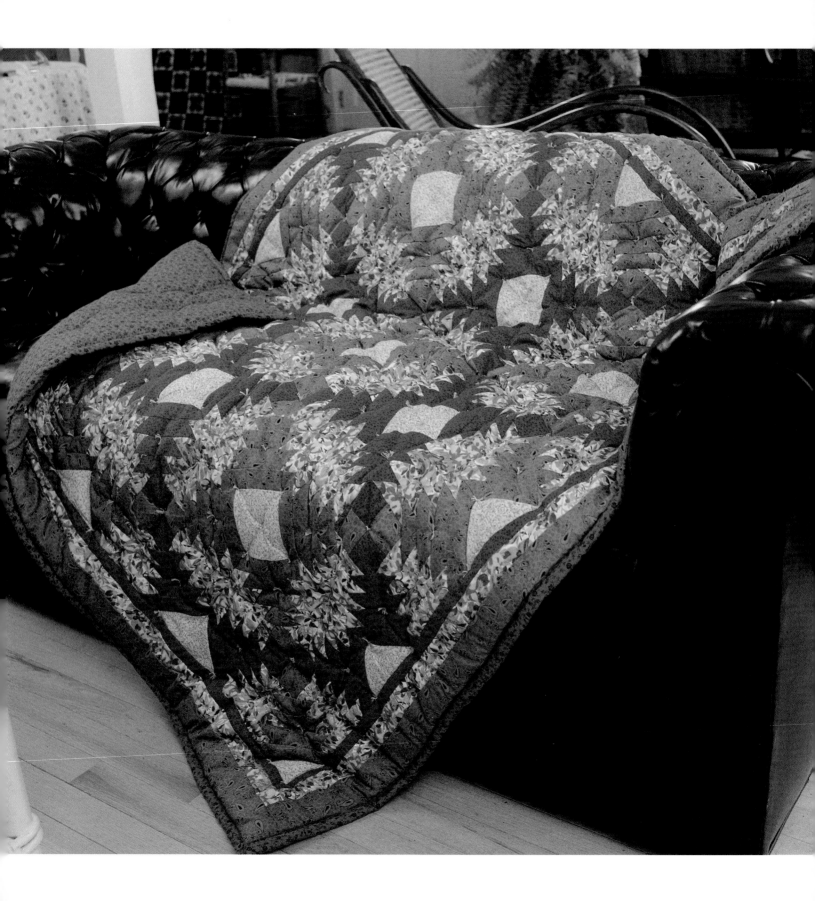

32 A
32 C
32 E
32 G
32 I
from green calico:
   2 strips, each 2½ × 48½ inches (top and bottom borders)
   2 strips, each 2½ × 52½ inches (side borders)
   32 A
   32 C
   32 E
   32 G
   32 I
from floral print:
   2 strips, each 2 × 45½ inches (top and bottom borders)
   2 strips, each 2 × 48½ inches (side borders)
   64 B
   64 D
   64 F
   64 H
from brown calico:
   1 piece, 45 × 55 inches (backing)
   1 piece, 10 × 55 inches (backing)

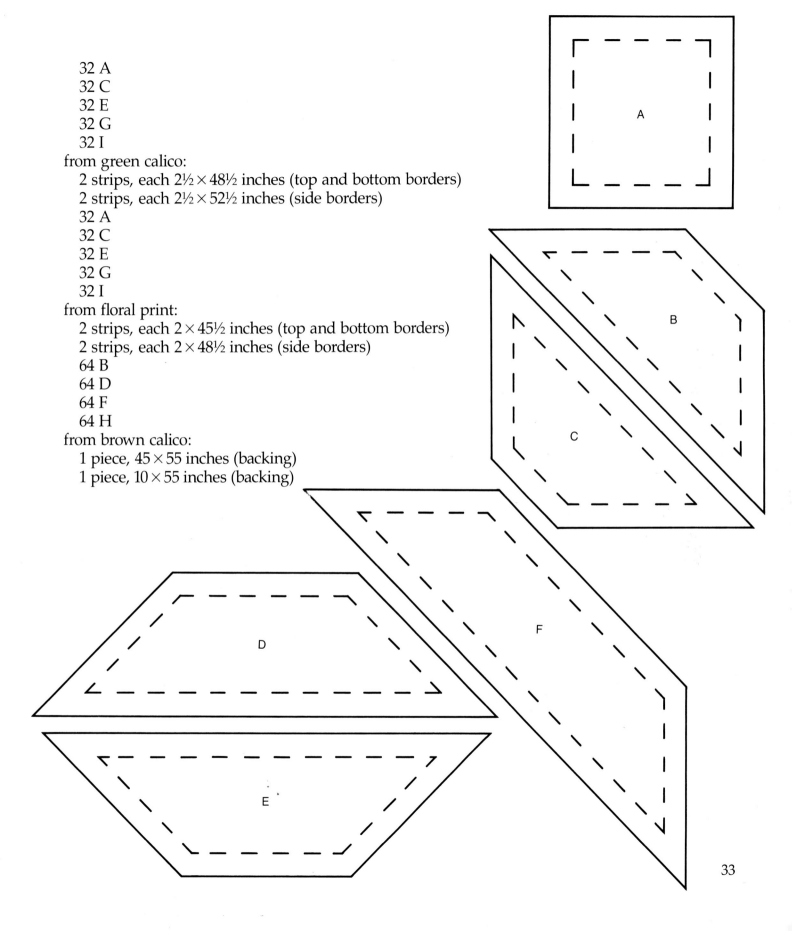

33

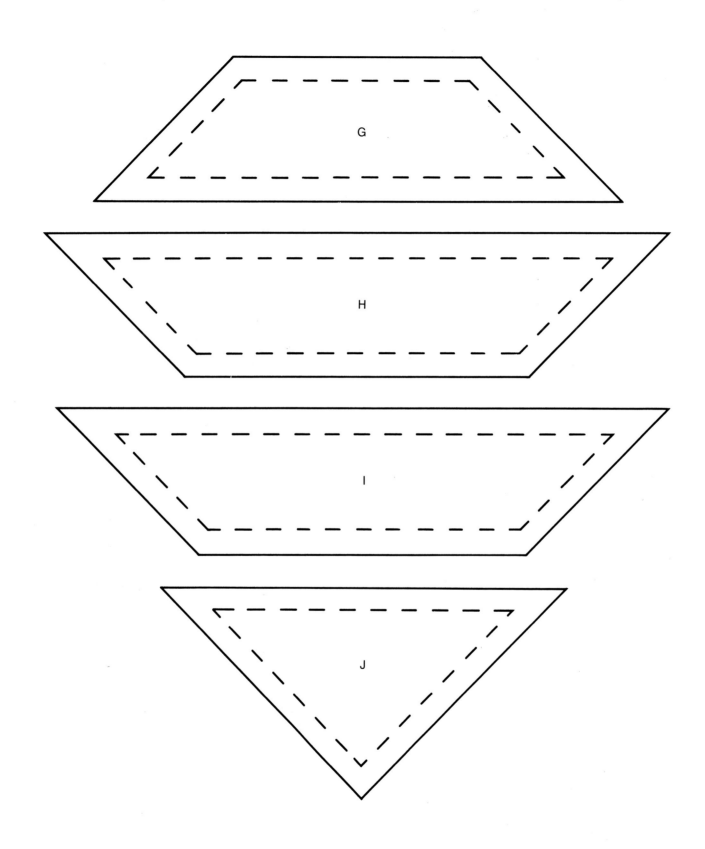

DIRECTIONS

To make a block

1. Refer to Figure 1. With right sides facing, join a green A piece to a rust A piece to make a rectangle as shown.
2. Press seams to one side. Make 2 rectangles in this way.
3. Refer to Figure 2. Join the 2 rectangles together to make a square as shown. Press seams to one side.
4. Refer to Figure 3. With right sides facing, join the long edge of a floral B piece to each side of the square. Press seams to one side.
5. Refer to Figure 4. With right sides facing, join the long edge of a green C piece to the top left corner and the bottom right corner.
6. Next, join a rust C piece to the other two corner edges as shown. Press seams to one side.
7. Refer to Figure 5. With right sides facing, join a floral D piece to each side of this unit as shown. Press seams to one side.
8. Using the green E pieces and rust E pieces, repeat step 5 as shown.
9. Refer to Figure 6. Continue in this way with the floral F pieces, then the green and rust G pieces, then the floral H pieces and ending with the green and rust I pieces.
10. With right sides facing, join the long edge of the tan J pieces to each corner to finish the block.
11. Press all seams to one side. Make 16 blocks in this way.

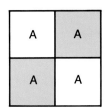

Figure 1

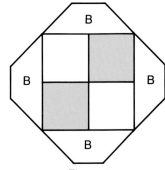

Figure 2

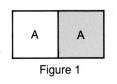

Figure 3

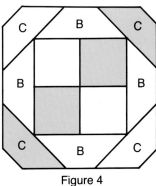

Figure 4

Figure 5

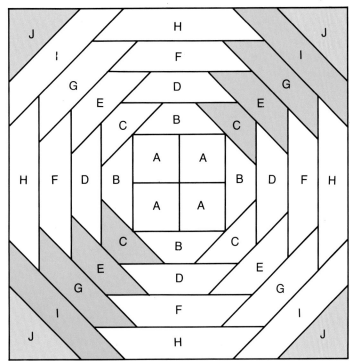

Figure 6

35

Figure 7

To join blocks

Refer to Figure 7.

1. Arrange the blocks into 4 rows of 4 blocks each as shown. *Note:* Every other block is turned so the rust and the green are in opposite directions.

2. With right sides facing, join all 4 blocks in each row.

3. Press seams to one side.

To join rows

Refer to Figure 7.

1. With right sides facing and seams aligned, join the bottom edge of the first row to the top edge of the second row.

2. Continue to join all 4 rows in this way.

3. Press seams to one side.

To join borders

Refer to Figure 7.

1. With right sides facing, join one of the shorter rust border strips to the top edge of the quilt top. Press seams to one side.
2. Repeat on the bottom edge of the quilt top in the same way.
3. Next, join one of the remaining rust border strips to each side of the quilt top in the same way.
4. With right sides facing, join one of the shorter floral border strips to the top edge of the quilt top and the other shorter floral strip to the bottom edge. Press seams to one side.
5. With right sides facing, join the remaining floral border strips to the sides of the quilt top. Press seams to one side.
6. With right sides facing, join the shorter green border strips to the top and bottom edges of the quilt top in the same way.
7. Join the remaining green border strips to the sides of the quilt top. Press seams to one side.

To prepare backing

1. With right sides facing, join the 10×55-inch backing piece along one long edge of the 45×55-inch backing piece.
2. Press seams to one side.

To tie quilt

1. With wrong sides facing and batting between, pin backing, batting, and quilt top all together.
2. See page 16 for tying instructions. Using the embroidery floss, tie the quilt in the center of each block and at evenly spaced intervals in each block.

To finish

1. Trim the quilt batting to the same size as the quilt top all around.
2. Fold the raw edges of the backing fabric forward ¼ inch and press.
3. Bring the remaining backing fabric forward to create a ½-inch border all around the quilt top and press.
4. Pin and slip-stitch all around to finish.

Kitchen Kapers

Blue-and-white gingham or homespun fabric is often used to make country accessories. It's especially crisp-looking in the kitchen. The fabric used here is from the Waverly Flower Patch Collection and is called Garden Check.

The curtains are a patchwork made from large squares, which makes it easy to adapt the directions for any size curtain needed to fit your windows. Each panel should measure the exact width of the window. The matching tablecloth is made from smaller squares and you simply add the number of rows needed to fit your table. The pattern is easily adaptable for making a runner or place mats as well. The pig-shaped tie-on chair backs can be made as place mats for another country accessory.

Patchwork Curtains

MATERIALS

Since all windows are different, measure the width and height of your windows, double this, then add 3 inches each for the top and bottom hems, another 2 inches for each side hem, and a little extra for the ¼-inch seam allowance on each side of all the patchwork squares. Divide this amount in half and purchase equal amounts of white solid fabric and blue-and-white checked fabric. You will also need white solid fabric to back each curtain. The amount needed will be twice the measurement of your window width by the length plus a few inches.

DIRECTIONS

Note: All measurements include a ¼-inch seam allowance.

To make rows

1. Cut each of the fabrics into 6½-inch squares. If your windows are small, you might want to make the squares 4½ × 4½ inches.
2. Alternating blue-and-white checked squares and white squares, arrange as many squares per row and as many rows as needed to make each curtain panel.
3. With right sides facing and raw edges aligned, join a blue-and-white checked square to a white square, then join a blue-and-white checked square, and so on until you have completed a row. Continue to make rows in this way.

To join rows

1. With right sides facing and all seams aligned, join the rows of alternating squares.
2. Press seams toward the blue-and-white checked squares so the check fabric doesn't show through the white squares.

To finish

1. For each panel, cut a same-sized piece of backing fabric.
2. With right sides facing, pin the pieced top and the backing fabric together.

3. Stitch around all edges, leaving a few inches open at the top for turning.

4. Clip the corners and turn right side out. Press.

5. Measure down 1 inch and stitch across the top of the curtains. Measure down another 1½ inches and stitch across to create a channel for the curtain rod. Pick open the seam at each end of each channel.

Patchwork Valance

Make the patchwork valance as you did the curtains. For added interest, you can stitch a panel of lace to the underside of the valance so it extends as much as you'd like below the valance edge.

Patchwork Tablecloth

Each square in this tablecloth measures 3 × 3 inches. If you'd like to change the size of the cover to fit your table, it's easy to do by adjusting the number of squares in each row and by adding or subtracting rows. The tablecloth shown here is 48 × 48 inches.

MATERIALS

Note: Yardages are figured for fabric 45 inches wide.

¾ yard blue-and-white checked fabric

¾ yard white solid fabric

1½ yards blue solid fabric (backing)

1½ yards thin quilt batting

optional: 5½ yards 1-inch-wide double-fold seam binding

CUTTING LIST

Note: All fabric measurements include a ¼-inch seam allowance.

Cut the following:

from blue-and-white check:
   64 squares, each 3½ × 3½ inches
from white solid:
   64 squares, each 3½ × 3½ inches

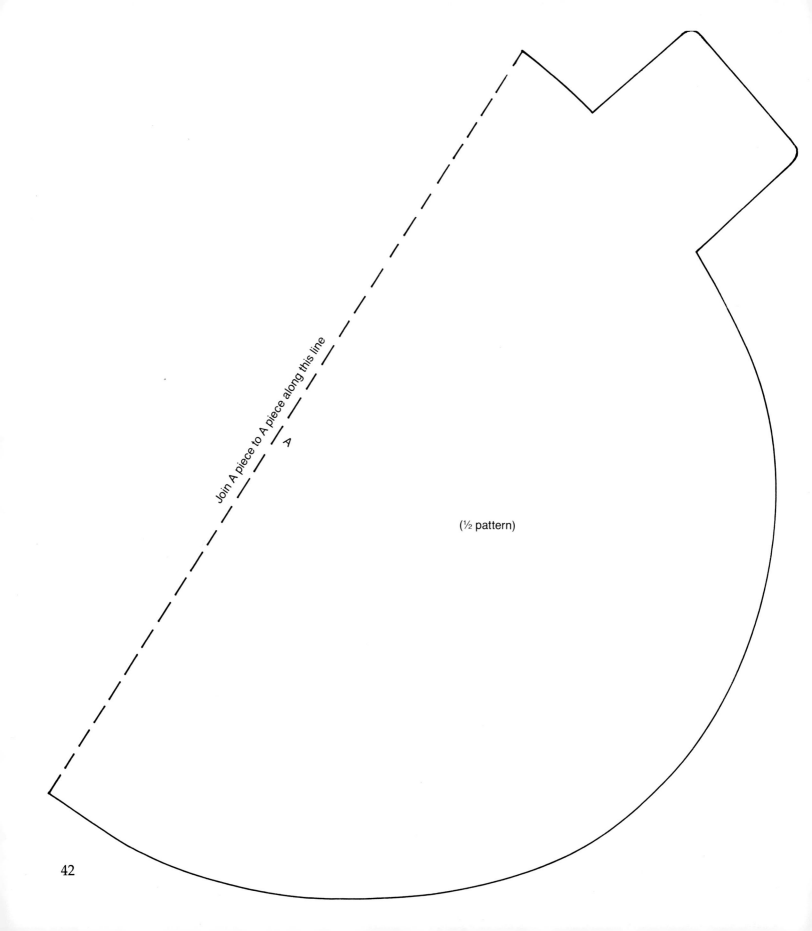

Join A piece to A piece along this line

A

(½ pattern)

42

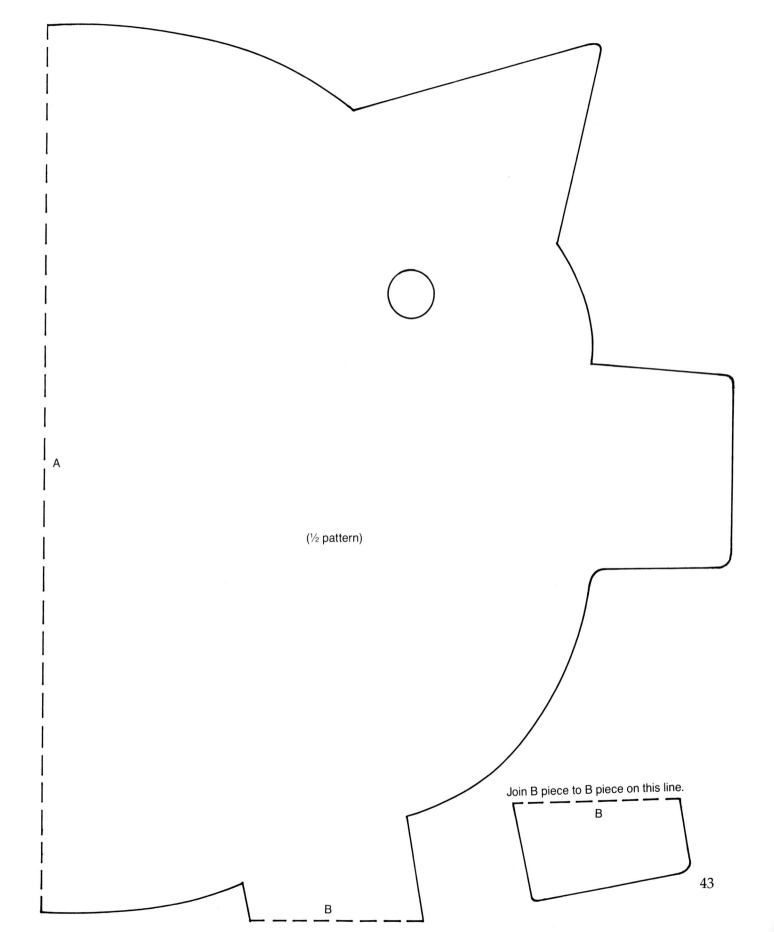

A

(½ pattern)

Join B piece to B piece on this line.

B

B

B

43

DIRECTIONS

To make rows

1. With right sides facing, join a blue-and-white checked square with a white square along one side edge.
2. Press seams to checked side.
3. Continue to join squares, alternating checked and white squares, to make a row of 16 squares. Press seams to checked side.
4. Make 16 rows in this way.

To join rows

1. Arrange the rows so the first row starts with a checked square, the second with a white square, and continue to alternate in this way.
2. With right sides facing and seams aligned, join the bottom edge of the first row to the edge of the second row.
3. Press seams to one side.
4. Continue to join all rows in this way.

To prepare backing

1. Begin by cutting 3½ inches off the bottom long edge of the blue solid fabric.
2. With right sides facing, pin this piece to one side edge of the larger piece of backing fabric.
3. Stitch together and trim to make a backing piece 48 × 48 inches. Open seams and press.

To quilt

1. With wrong sides facing and batting between, pin backing, batting, and patchwork top together.
2. Starting at the center and working outward in a sunburst pattern, take long, loose basting stitches through all 3 layers.
3. Using small running stitches, quilt ¼ inch on each side of all seam lines. Do not stitch into the ¼-inch seam allowance all around the top.

To finish

1. Trim the batting ¼ inch all around.
2. Turn the raw edges of the quilt top and the backing to the inside ¼ inch and press.
3. Machine-stitch all around to close open edges or encase the raw edges inside solid blue seam binding for a narrow blue band all around the quilt top. Slip-stitch all around.

Barnyard Chair Backs

These chair backs can be made to use as place mats if desired. Simply leave off the ties. The finished size of the seat backs is 10 × 14 inches.

CUTTING LIST

Note: All measurements include a ¼-inch seam allowance. Trace the pig pattern aligning matching dash lines. Cut out the pattern and use it to cut the fabric.

Cut the following:

from blue-and-white check:
 8 pig patterns with an added ¼-inch seam allowance
 8 strips, each 1½ × 18 inches
from quilt batting:
 4 pig patterns without seam allowance

DIRECTIONS

To make chair back

1. With right sides facing and batting on top, pin backing, batting, and top pieces together.
2. Stitch around the outside edge, leaving the top 6½ inches open for turning.
3. Trim the seam allowance and clip into it around all curved edges and into corners on each side of the snout and the legs.
4. Turn right side out and use the eraser end of a pencil or another blunt instrument to push out the ends of the ears, snout, and legs.

To finish

1. Turn the raw edges of each of the 8 strips to the inside ¼ inch and press.
2. With wrong sides facing, fold the strips in half lengthwise and press.
3. Stitch together along all edges.
4. Fold each strip in half and insert the fold of the 2 strips between the front and the back of the pig at each end of the open edge.
5. Turn the raw edges of the front and the back to the inside and press. Pin together and machine-stitch the opening closed as close to the edge as possible.
6. Attach the button in position on the front of the pig as shown on the pattern.

Materials (for 4 chair backs)
Note: Yardages are figured for fabric 45 inches wide.
1½ yards blue-and-white checked fabric
1 yard thin quilt batting
4 black buttons for eyes
tracing paper

Fanfare

Every stitcher eventually amasses a basket filled with scraps. I don't know why, but it's impossible to throw away even the tiniest remnant on the chance that it may someday be used. Perhaps this fact accounts for the popularity of the scrap quilt. It's a chance to use up the variety of fabrics and justify saving fabric pieces.

This fan pattern was repeated to make a 76 × 86-inch quilt to fit a double or queen-size bed. If you want to make a single-bed quilt, it's easy to do by eliminating rows.

MATERIALS
Note: Yardages are figured for fabric 45 inches wide.
a good variety of calico fabrics
2½ yards blue solid fabric
8 yards white solid fabric (includes backing)
quilt batting 80 × 90 inches
tracing paper
cardboard

CUTTING LIST
Note: All measurements include a ¼-inch seam allowance. Trace patterns A, B, and, C and transfer them to cardboard for templates (see page 13).

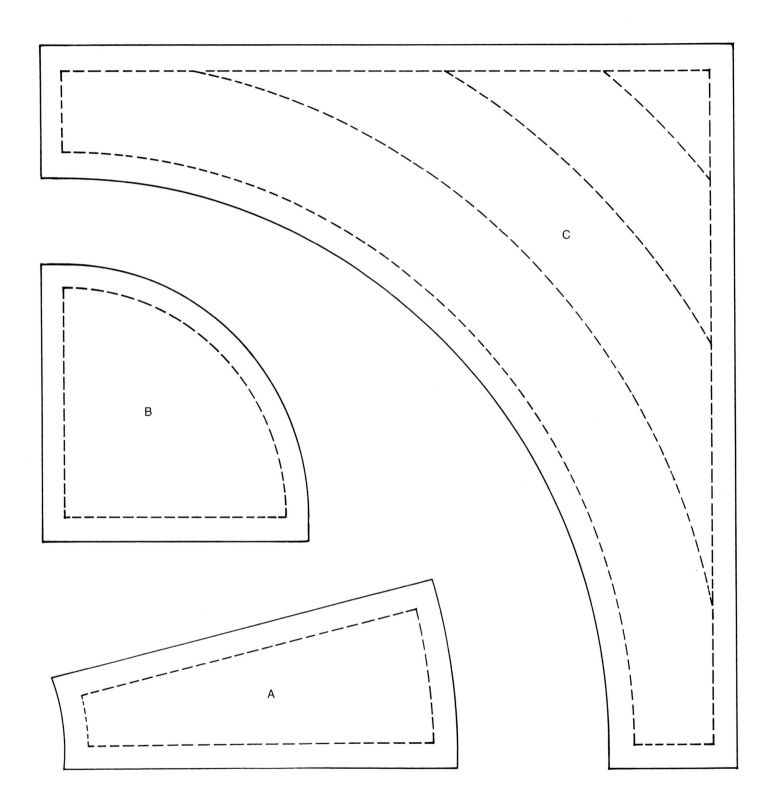

Cut the following:

from calicos:

   686 A

from blue solid:

   2 strips, each 3 × 85½ inches (side borders)

   2 strips, each 3 × 70½ inches (top and bottom borders)

   98 B

from white solid:

   2 pieces, each 45 × 80 inches (backing)

   98 C

   13 squares, each 7⅞ × 7⅞ inches (Cut each square along the diagonal to make 2 triangles each, for a total of 26 triangles.)

   1 square, 8¼ × 8¼ inches (Cut square along the diagonal in both directions to make 4 triangles.)

DIRECTIONS

To make a block

1. Refer to Figure 1. With right sides facing, join a calico A piece to another calico A piece along one long edge.

2. Press seams to one side.

3. With right sides facing, continue to join 7 calico A pieces in this way to form an arc. Press seams to one side.

4. Refer to Figure 2. With right sides facing, join the curve of a blue B piece (base of fan) to the inside curve of the fan spokes (A pieces) as shown.

5. Press seams to one side.

6. Refer to Figure 3. With right sides facing, join the curve of a white C piece to the outside curve of the fan spokes (A pieces) as shown to complete the fan block.

7. Press seams to one side. Make 98 blocks in this way.

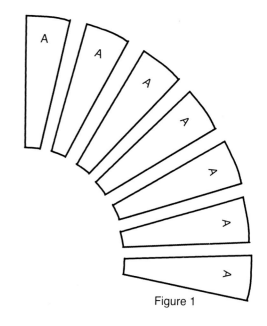

Figure 1

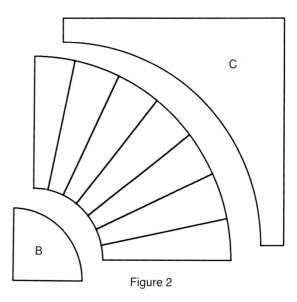

Figure 2

Figure 3

49

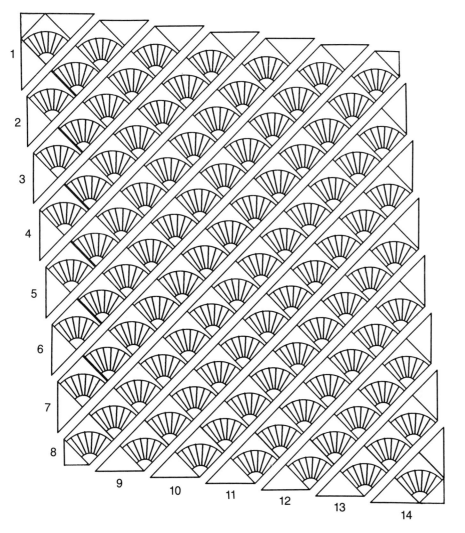

Figure 4

To join blocks

Refer to Figure 4.

Note: Blocks are set on the diagonal.

1. Arrange blocks and white triangles into 14 rows as shown.

2. With right sides facing, join a large white triangle to one side edge of the fan block in Row 1 as shown. Press seams to one side.

3. Next, join another triangle to the opposite side of the fan block in Row 1 in the same way.

4. Then join the long edge of a small white triangle to the top edge of the fan block in Row 1. Press seams to one side.

5. For Row 2, with right sides facing, join one side edge of a white triangle to the side edge of a block, followed by 2 more blocks, and end with a white triangle as shown. Press seams to one side.

6. Continue to join the blocks with the white triangles at the ends of each row through Row 6. Join a small white triangle at the end of Row 7 and a small white triangle at the opposite end of Row 8 as shown.

7. Then continue to join a large white triangle at the beginning and end of Rows 9 through 14, ending with a small white triangle at the bottom of Row 14.

8. Press seams to one side.

To join rows

Refer to Figure 5.

1. With right sides facing and seams aligned, stitch the bottom edge of Row 1 to the top edge of Row 2. Press seams to one side.

2. Continue to join all 14 rows in this way to make the quilt top.

3. Press seams to one side.

51

Figure 5

To join borders

Refer to Figure 5.

1. With right sides facing, join one of the shorter blue border strips to the top edge of the quilt.
2. Repeat with the other short blue border strip across the bottom edge of the quilt top.
3. Press seams to one side.
4. With right sides facing, join one remaining blue border strip to each side edge of the quilt top.
5. Press seams to one side.

To prepare backing

1. With right sides facing, stitch the 2 backing pieces together down one long side.
2. Press seams to one side.

To quilt

Refer to page 13 for directions for tracing and transferring patterns.

1. Trace the quilting pattern and transfer it to the white areas of the quilt.
2. With wrong sides facing, and batting between, pin the backing, batting, and quilt top together.
3. Beginning at the center and working outward in a sunburst pattern, take long, loose basting stitches through all 3 layers, stopping short of the seam allowance all around the outside edge.
4. Using small running stitches, quilt on all premarked lines.

To finish

1. When all the quilting is complete, remove the basting stitches.
2. Trim the batting to ¼ inch smaller than the quilt top all around.
3. Trim the backing so that it is 1 inch larger than the quilt top all around.
4. Fold the backing edges to the inside ¼ inch and press. Then fold the edges over again onto the front of the quilt top to form a ½-inch border all around. Press and pin.
5. Slip-stitch the border to the quilt top to finish.

Color-Wheel Pillows

*While each of these pillows is a distinctly
different pattern, they look good together
because the same colors were used for each.
These are perfect scrap projects. The designs
will look best if you choose light and dark
colors. Each pattern is created from long strips
of fabric. As you add each color strip to build
the design you cut away the excess length of
the previous strip.*

MATERIALS

Pillow 1
Note: You will need small amounts of the colors listed. Refer
to the cutting lists to cut the largest pieces before cutting
the remainder into strips.
 scraps of fabric in the following colors: red (A), yellow (B),
  tan (C), pink (D), purple (E), pale blue (F), dark green
  (G), light green (H), royal blue (I), light blue (J), brown
  (K), dark pink (L), and dark slate blue (M).
 backing fabric 18½ × 18½ inches
 2 yards piping
 stuffing or 18 × 18-inch pillow form

THE BASKET COLLECTORS BOOK

Larason

54

Pillow 2
- a variety of fabric scraps in 11 different colors to make 1½-inch-wide strips for the equivalent of 60 inches long for each color. The length does not have to be in one continuous strip. You will need the following colors: yellow (A), pink (B), pale blue (C), light green (D), coral (E), ochre (F), purple (G), navy (H), red (I), dark green (J), dark slate blue (K).
- backing fabric 18½ × 18½ inches
- 2 yards piping
- stuffing or 18 × 18-inch pillow form

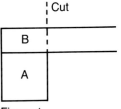

Figure 1

CUTTING LIST

Note: All measurements include a ¼-inch seam allowance.

Pillow 1
Cut the following:

from red (A):
   1 square, 2½ × 2½ inches
   2 strips, each 1½ × 18½ inches (top and bottom borders)
   2 strips, each 1½ × 16½ inches (side borders)
from yellow (B):
   1 piece, 11 × 13 inches
from dark slate blue (M):
   1 piece, 11 × 13 inches
from all:
   strips 1½ inches wide by approximately 20–30 inches long.

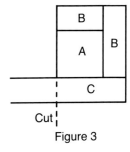

Figure 2

DIRECTIONS
Pillow 1

To make pillow top
1. Refer to Figure 1. With right sides facing, join the red (A) square to one end of a yellow (B) strip as shown.
2. Cut away the excess B fabric.
3. Press seam to one side.
4. Next, refer to Figure 2 and, with right sides facing, join the yellow (B) strip to the right side edge of this piece as shown.
5. Cut away the excess B fabric. Press seam to one side.
6. Refer to Figure 3 and, with right sides facing, join the tan (C) strip to the bottom edge of the pieced square as shown.

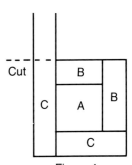

Figure 3

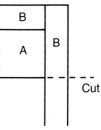

Figure 4

55

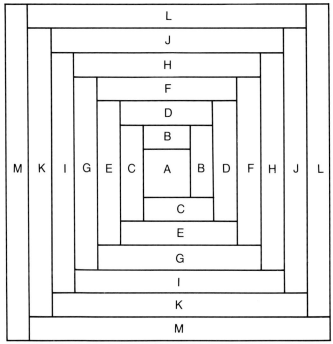

Figure 5

7. Cut away the excess C fabric. Press seam to one side.

8. Refer to Figure 4 and, with right sides facing, join the tan (C) strip to the left side edge of the pieced square as shown.

9. Cut away the excess C fabric. Press seam to one side.

10. Refer to Figure 5 and continue to add strips in the colors indicated.

To make borders

The blue and yellow sawtooth border is made with the quick-and-easy method (see page 16).

1. On the wrong side of the 11×13-inch yellow (B) fabric, measure and mark a grid of 5 rows of 6 squares each, $1\frac{7}{8} \times 1\frac{7}{8}$ inches.

2. With right sides facing, pin the marked fabric to the 11×13-inch dark slate blue (M) fabric.

3. Refer to page 16 for stitching and cutting instructions. You will have 60 squares.

4. With right sides facing, join 2 pieced squares along one side edge. Press seams to one side.

5. Continue to join squares, making sure all the colors are facing in the same direction, to make a strip of 14 squares. Repeat to make a second strip.

6. Join squares to make a strip of 16 squares for the side border. Make another strip.

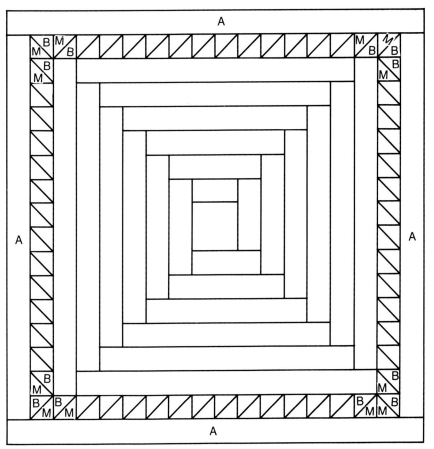

Pillow 1   Figure 6

7. Refer to Figure 6. With right sides facing, join the shorter pieced borders to the top and bottom edges of the pillow top. Press seams to one side.

8. Repeat with the sawtooth side borders.

9. Next, join a shorter red border strip to each side edge of the pillow top. Press seams to one side.

10. Repeat with the longer red border strips on the top and bottom edges of the pillow top. Press seams to one side.

To finish

1. With right sides facing and raw edges aligned, pin the piping to the pillow top and stitch around.

2. With right sides facing, pin the backing fabric to the pillow top and, using the piping stitches as a guide, sew around 4 corners and 3 sides.

3. Clip the corners and trim the seam allowance.

4. Turn pillow right side out and press.

5. Fill with stuffing or insert purchased pillow form and turn raw edges to the inside. Press.

6. Slip-stitch the opening closed.

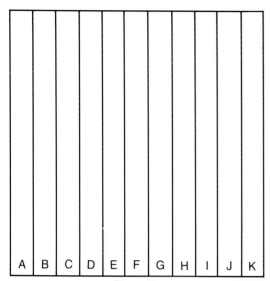

A | B | C | D | E | F | G | H | I | J | K

Figure 7

Figure 8

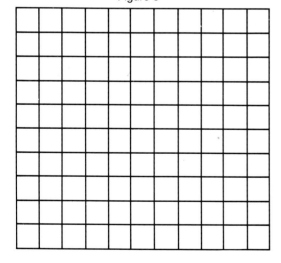

A | B | C | D | E | F | G | H | I | J | K

Key

A Yellow   G Purple
B Pink   H Navy
C Pale Blue   I Red
D Light Green   J Dark Green
E Coral   K Dark Slate
F Ochre

Pillow 2

To make rows

1. With right sides facing, pin all strips together in the sequence shown in Figure 7. To keep the unit from curving, stitch each strip in the opposite direction from the previous one and press after each addition.

2. Measure and draw lines across the strips every 1½ inches. Cut along these lines as shown in Figure 8.

To join rows in each block

Refer to Figure 9.

1. Beginning with the bottom row of the upper right block, remove the dark green (J) and dark slate blue (K) squares from one strip by pulling out the thread that joins them to the row.

2. Remove the yellow (A) square from the beginning of the next row up and the dark slate blue (K) squares from the end of that row in the same way and add them to the end of the 4th row up.

3. Continue to remove and add squares according to the diagram to complete each block section.

To join blocks

Refer to Figure 9.

1. With right sides facing and matching all seams where they will be joined, stitch the upper left and upper right blocks together along the side edge.

2. Press seams to one side.

3. Join the lower left and lower right blocks in the same way.

4. With right sides facing and matching all seams where they will be joined, stitch the upper and lower sections together along one long edge.

5. Press seams to one side to complete the pillow top.

To finish

Refer to the instructions for Pillow 1 (page 57) and finish in the same way.

F	E	D	C	B	A	K	J
E	D	C	B	A	K	J	I
D	C	B	A	K	J	I	H
C	B	A	K	J	I	H	G
B	A	K	J	I	H	G	F
A	K	J	I	H	G	F	E
K	J	I	H	G	F	E	D
J	I	H	G	F	E	D	C
I	H	G	F	E	D	C	B

I	J	K	A	B	C	D	E	F
H	I	J	K	A	B	C	D	E
G	H	I	J	K	A	B	C	D
F	G	H	I	J	K	A	B	C
E	F	G	H	I	J	K	A	B
D	E	F	G	H	I	J	K	A
C	D	E	F	G	H	I	J	K
B	C	D	E	F	G	H	I	J
A	B	C	D	E	F	G	H	I

Pillow 2
Figure 9

J	I	H	G	F	E	D	C
K	J	I	H	G	F	E	D
A	K	J	I	H	G	F	E
B	A	K	J	I	H	G	F
C	B	A	K	J	I	H	G
D	C	B	A	K	J	I	H
E	D	C	B	A	K	J	I
F	E	D	C	B	A	K	J

B	C	D	E	F	G	H	I	J
C	D	E	F	G	H	I	J	K
D	E	F	G	H	I	J	K	A
E	F	G	H	I	J	K	A	B
F	G	H	I	J	K	A	B	C
G	H	I	J	K	A	B	C	D
H	I	J	K	A	B	C	D	E
I	J	K	A	B	C	D	E	F

Chloe's Star Quilt

Star patterns are attractive designs to make from bold contrasting fabrics or from a multitude of colorful scraps. This was a common practice among early quiltmakers and we often see antique quilts of this nature. This delightful country quilt is used on a painted iron bed in a young girl's bedroom. The quilt background is sunshine yellow covered with a simple grid of quilting stitches in the solid areas. The finished measurement is 48 × 62 inches.

MATERIALS
Note: Yardages are figured for fabric 45 inches wide.
a variety of print scraps
4½ yards yellow solid fabric
quilt batting 48 × 62 inches
tracing paper
cardboard
quilt marking pen

CUTTING LIST
Note: All measurements include a ¼-inch seam allowance.
Trace patterns A, B, and C and transfer them to cardboard
   for templates (see page 13).

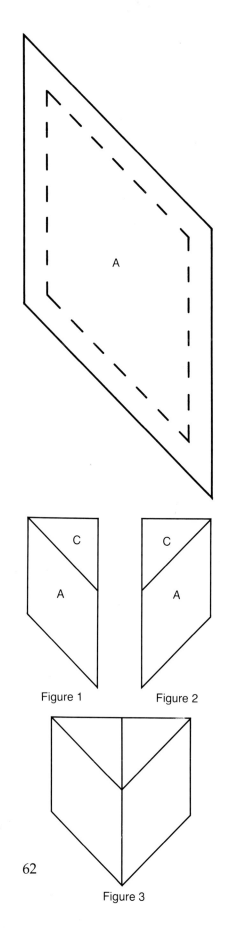

A

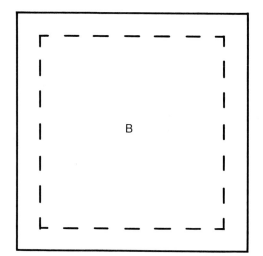

B

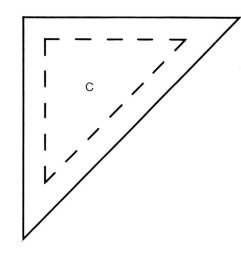

C

Cut the following:

from prints:

384 A

from yellow solid:

1 piece, 45 × 66 inches (backing)

2 strips, each 4½ × 66 inches (backing)

2 strips, each 3½ × 62½ inches (side borders)

2 strips, each 3½ × 42½ inches (top and bottom borders)

192 B

384 C

To make a block

1. Refer to Figure 1. With right sides facing, join the diagonal edge of a yellow C piece to a print A piece as shown.

2. Press seams to one side. Make 4 pieces in this way.

3. Refer to Figure 2. With right sides facing, join the diagonal edge of a yellow C piece to a print A piece as shown. (This is a reverse of Figure 1.)

4. Press seams to one side. Make 4 pieces in this way.

5. Refer to Figure 3. With right sides facing, join a piece made in Figure 1 to a piece made in Figure 2 along the long edge as shown.

6. Press seams to one side. Make 4 sections in this way.

To assemble block

1. Refer to Figure 4. Arrange the 4 sections made in Figure 3 as shown.

2. Refer to Figure 5. With right sides facing, stitch all 4 sections together to make the star as shown.

C

A

Figure 1

C

A

Figure 2

62

Figure 3

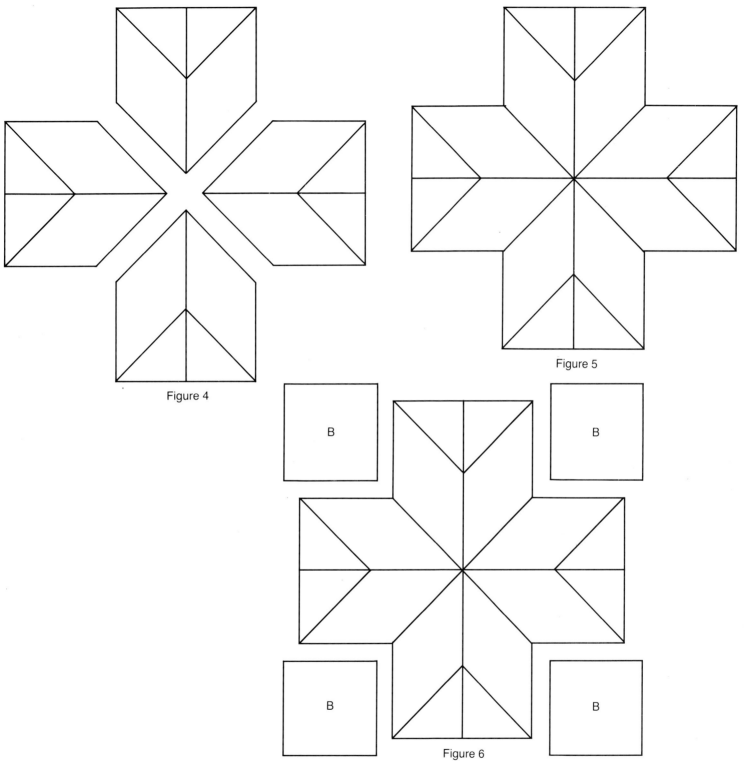

Figure 4

Figure 5

B

B

B

B

Figure 6

3. Press seams to one side.
4. Refer to Figure 6. With right sides facing, join a yellow B piece to each corner of the star in the following way: Starting at the outside edge, stitch toward the inner corner of the

yellow B piece. Leaving the needle in the fabric, lift the presser foot on your machine and turn the fabric. Then stitch down the other side to the outer edge. This is the quilt block.

5. Press seams to one side. Make 48 blocks in this way.

To join blocks

Refer to Figure 7.

1. With right sides facing, join 2 blocks along the right side edge.

2. Press seams to one side.

3. Continue to join 4 more blocks in this way to make a row.

4. Make 8 rows in this way.

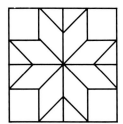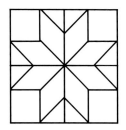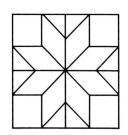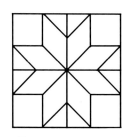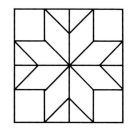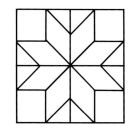

Figure 7

To join rows

Refer to Figure 8.

1. With right sides facing, join the bottom edge of the first row to the top edge of the second row.

2. Press seams to one side.

3. Continue to join all 8 rows in this way.

To join borders

1. With right sides facing, join one of the shorter yellow border strips across the top edge of the quilt. Repeat with the other shorter yellow border strip across the bottom edge of the quilt top.

2. Press seams to one side.

3. With right sides facing, join one of the remaining yellow border strips to each side edge of the quilt top.

4. Press seams to one side.

Figure 8

65

To prepare backing

1. With right sides facing, join one of the 4½ × 66-inch backing strips to each long side edge of the 45 × 66-inch backing piece.
2. Press seams to one side.

To quilt

Note: The quilting stitches cover the entire quilt in a diagonal grid. However, if you prefer, you can simply mark lines across the solid background areas of the quilt and plan to quilt the star blocks along the seam lines. To mark entire quilt:

1. Place a yardstick on the diagonal across one corner of the quilt top and draw a line. Without lifting the yardstick, turn it over on the fabric and mark another line.
2. Continue to mark evenly spaced lines across the entire quilt in this way.
3. If you want to quilt only the background and not the pieced stars, mark these areas only.
4. With wrong sides facing and batting between, pin the backing fabric, batting, and quilt top together.
5. Beginning at the center and working outward in a sunburst pattern, take long, loose, basting stitches through all 3 layers of fabric.
6. Using small running stitches, quilt along all premarked lines, stopping short of the seam allowance around the outside edges of the quilt top. To quilt the star blocks, take small running stitches ¼ inch on each side of all pieced seam lines.

To finish

1. Trim the batting ¼ inch smaller than the quilt top all around.
2. Turn the raw edges of the backing and the quilt top to the inside and press.
3. Pin together and machine-stitch all around to finish the quilt.

Crossroads Quilt

While this is a traditional patchwork design, the geometric pattern can look quite contemporary. It is an interesting pattern because the blocks create an optical illusion. All sewn lines are straight, but the squares don't always look parallel. This pastel interpretation was made by Karen Schwenk. It measures 61 × 89 inches to fit a single bed.

MATERIALS
Note: Yardages are figured for fabric 45 inches wide.
½ yard lavender solid fabric for binding
1½ yards pale lavender/blue print (A)
1½ yards dark lavender print (B)
2½ yards blue print (C)
2 yards light purple solid (border)
2¼ yards light blue solid (border)
3½ yards pastel print (backing)
batting 61 × 89 inches
1 skein lavender embroidery floss for tying
tracing paper
cardboard

CUTTING LIST
Note: All measurements include a ¼-inch seam allowance.
Trace patterns X and Y and transfer them to cardboard for
  templates (see page 13).

Cut the following:

from lavender solid:

    7 strips, each 2 × 45 inches cut on the bias

      from pale lavender/blue print (A):

    120 Y

from dark lavender print (B):

    64 X

    84 Y

from blue print (C):

    (Cut border strips vertically before cutting Y pieces.)

    2 strips, each 4½ × 80½ inches (side borders)

    2 strips, each 4½ × 60½ inches (top and bottom borders)

    148 Y

from light purple solid:

    2 strips, each 2½ × 70½ inches (side borders)

    2 strips, each 2½ × 46½ inches (top and bottom borders)

from light blue solid:

    2 strips, each 3½ × 74½ inches (side borders)

    2 strips, each 3½ × 52½ inches (top and bottom borders)

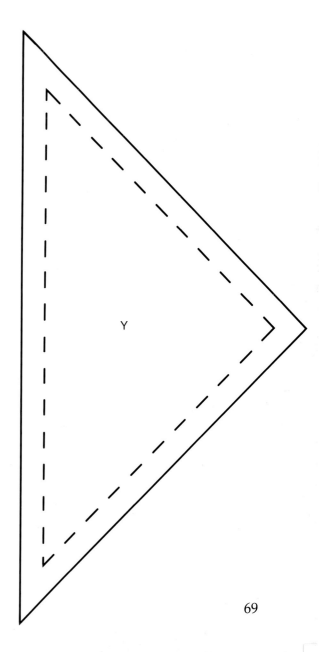

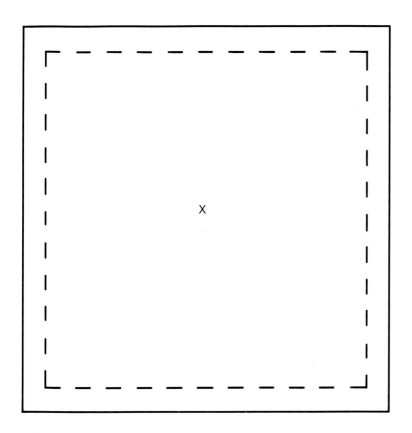

Figure 1

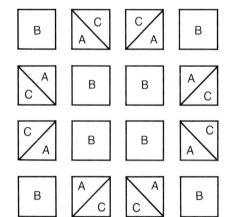

Figure 2

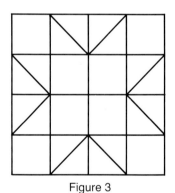

Figure 3

DIRECTIONS

To make Block 1

1. Refer to Figure 1. With right sides facing and raw edges aligned, stitch a pale lavender/blue print (A) Y piece to a blue print (C) Y piece along the diagonal to make a square.

2. Press seams to one side. Make 8 squares in this way.

3. Refer to Figure 2 and arrange the 8 pieced squares and 8 of the dark lavender (B) squares into 4 rows of 4 squares each as shown.

4. With right sides facing, stitch the 4 squares together in each row to make 4 rows.

5. Press seams to one side.

6. Refer to Figure 3. With right sides facing and seams aligned, stitch the bottom edge of the top row to the top edge of the second row. Continue to join all 4 rows in this way to make Block 1.

7. Press seams to one side. Make 8 blocks in this way.

To make Block 2

1. Refer to Figure 1. With right sides facing, stitch a pale lavender/blue print (A) Y piece to a blue print (C) Y piece along the diagonal to make a square as you did for Block 1.

2. Press seams to one side. Make 4 squares in this way.

3. With right sides facing, stitch a pale lavender/blue print

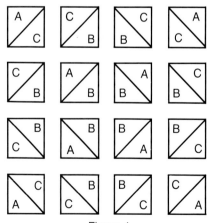

Figure 4

(A) Y piece to a dark lavender (B) Y piece to make a square.

4. Press seams to one side. Make 4 squares in this way.

5. With right sides facing, stitch a blue print (C) Y piece to a dark lavender print (B) Y piece to make a square.

6. Press seams to one side. Make 8 squares in this way.

7. Refer to Figure 4 and arrange these 16 pieced squares into 4 rows of 4 squares in each row as shown.

8. With right sides facing, stitch the 4 squares together in each row to make 4 rows.

9. Refer to Figure 5. With right sides facing and seams aligned, stitch the bottom edge of the top row to the top edge of the second row. Continue to join all 4 rows in this way to make Block 2.

10. Press seams to one side. Make 7 blocks in this way.

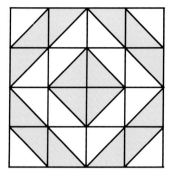

Figure 5

To join blocks

1. With right sides facing and seams aligned, stitch the right side edge of a Block 1 to the left side edge of a Block 2. Next, stitch the right side of the Block 2 to the left side edge of another Block 1 to make a row.

2. Press seams to one side. Make 3 rows in this way to make Rows 1, 3, and 5.

3. With right sides facing and seams aligned, stitch the right side edge of a Block 2 to the left side edge of a Block 1. Next, stitch the right side edge of the Block 1 to the left side edge of another Block 2 to make a row.

4. Press seams to one side. Make 2 rows in this way to make Rows 2 and 4.

To join rows

Refer to Figure 6.

1. With right sides facing and seams aligned, stitch the bottom edge of Row 1 to the top edge of Row 2.

2. Next, stitch the bottom edge of Row 2 to the top edge of Row 3.

3. Continue to join all 5 rows in this way to make the quilt top.

4. Press seams to one side.

To join borders

Refer to Figure 6.

1. With right sides facing, join one of the longer light purple border strips to each side edge of the quilt top.

Figure 6

2. Next, stitch the remaining 2 light purple border strips to the top and bottom edges of the quilt top. Press seams to one side.

3. With right sides facing, stitch the longer light blue border strips to the sides of the quilt top.

4. Next, stitch the remaining 2 light blue border strips to the top and bottom edges of the quilt top in the same way.

5. With right sides facing, join a longer blue print (C) border strip to each side of the quilt top.

6. Next, stitch the remaining 2 blue print (C) border strips to the top and bottom edges of the quilt top in the same way. Press all seams to one side.

To make backing and prepare quilt for tying

1. Cut the backing fabric in half crosswise so you have 2 pieces, each 45 × 63 inches.

2. With right sides facing, stitch the 2 pieces together along one long edge to make one piece 63 × 89½ inches. Open seams and press.

3. With wrong sides facing and batting between, pin the backing, batting, and quilt top together.

To tie the quilt

1. Cut the embroidery floss into 10-inch lengths.

2. Tie the quilt in the center of each block (see page 16).

3. Continue to make ties at the corners of each block and along the seam lines of the borders where the seams of each row intersect with the border.

To finish

1. Binding: With right sides facing, stitch the short ends of the 7 dark lavender strips together to make a long strip.

2. Fold the long side edges over onto the wrong side of the fabric so they meet in the center and press. Fold in half again and press.

3. Trim the batting and the backing to the same size as the quilt top.

4. Pin the binding around the quilt edges with all 3 layers between the fold of the binding. Fold the ends under where they meet at the end and tuck one end inside the other to finish.

5. Slip-stitch the binding to the quilt top on the front and back all around.

Bow Tie Quilt

My mother, Ruth Linsley, used scraps of fabric left over from other projects to make this pretty bow tie quilt. The quilt is tied rather than hand-quilted. It measures 66 × 90 inches to fit a single bed.

My friend Maddie Bohnsack sponge-painted the floor in her guest room with a lavender tint, then added feminine touches with painted furniture. A pitcher filled with flowers from the garden, a new seat cover on an old rocking chair, and a delightful antique lamp add to the room's old-fashioned country charm.

MATERIALS
Note: Yardages are figured for fabric 45 inches wide.
a variety of pastel calico fabrics
2¼ yards lavender calico
5¼ yards backing fabric
quilt batting 66 × 90 inches
1 skein blue embroidery floss for tying
tracing paper
cardboard

CUTTING LIST
Note: All measurements include a ¼-inch seam allowance.
Trace patterns A and B and transfer them to cardboard for templates (see page 13).

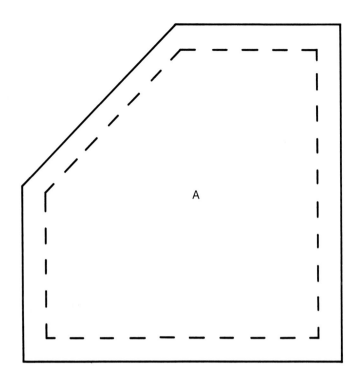

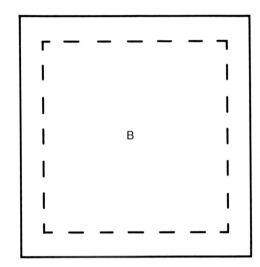

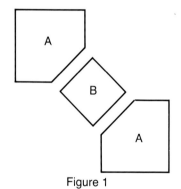

Figure 1

Cut the following:

from calicos:

> (There are 117 blocks. In each block, 2 of the A pieces and 1 of the B pieces should be of the same print.)
>
> 468 A
>
> 117 B

from lavender calico:

> 2 strips, each 6½ × 78½ inches (side borders)
>
> 2 strips, each 6½ × 66½ inches (top and bottom borders)

DIRECTIONS
To make blocks

1. Refer to Figure 1. With right sides facing, join a diagonal edge of a calico A piece to one side edge of a calico B piece of the same color. Press seams to one side.

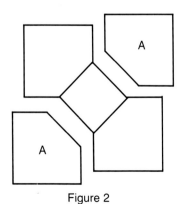

Figure 2

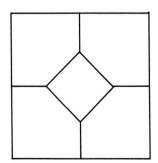

Figure 3

2. Repeat with another A piece of the same color on the opposite side of the calico B piece as shown.
3. Refer to Figure 2. Using 2 A pieces of the same color, but different from the colors used for the pieces in steps 1 and 2, join a calico A piece to each of the remaining sides of the A and B pieces to complete the box shown in Figure 3.
4. Press seams to one side. Make 117 blocks in this way.

To make rows

Refer to Figure 4.
1. Arrange blocks into 13 rows of 9 blocks each.
2. With right sides facing, join all 9 blocks in each row.
3. Press seams to one side.

To join rows

Refer to Figure 4.
1. With right sides facing, join the bottom edge of the first row to the top edge of the second row.
2. Press seams to one side.
3. Continue to join all 13 rows in this way.

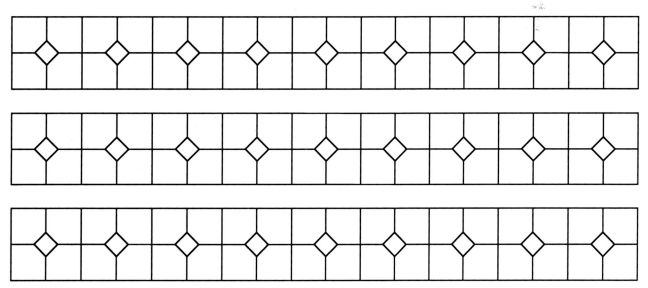

Figure 4

To join borders

Refer to Figure 5.

1. With right sides facing, join one of the longer lavender calico border strips to one side edge of the quilt top.
2. Press seams to one side.
3. Repeat on the opposite side edge of the quilt top.
4. Next, join the remaining lavender border strips to the top and bottom edges of the quilt top in the same way.

To prepare backing

1. Cut the backing fabric in half crosswise.
2. With right sides facing, join the 2 pieces along one long edge.
3. Press seams to one side.

To quilt

1. In the border areas, rule off lines 1 inch apart.
2. With wrong sides facing and batting between, pin the backing, batting, and quilt top together.
3. Beginning at the center and working outward in a sunburst pattern, take long, loose basting stitches through all 3 layers.
4. Using the blue embroidery floss, tie the quilt in the center of each block (see page 16).
5. Using small running stitches, quilt along the marked lines in the borders. Do not quilt into the seam allowance around the edges of the quilt.

To finish

1. Trim the batting ¼ inch smaller than the quilt top all around.
2. Trim the backing fabric to the same size as the quilt top.
3. Turn the edge of the quilt top and the backing to the inside ¼ inch and press.
4. Pin together and slip-stitch or machine-stitch all around to finish.

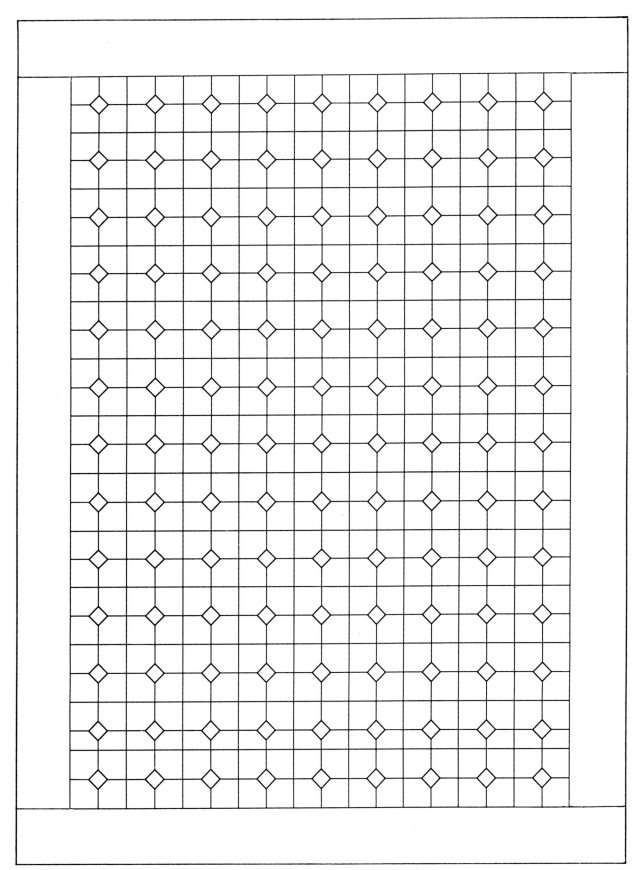

Figure 5

All in Bloom

Place mats and napkins are always appreciated as gifts. This project makes good use of pretty leftover fabric from quilts. A rectangle of floral print is used for the center of the place mat and the solid colors found in the print are used to create a patchwork border. The floral fabric is also used for the backing and for a narrow band around the top. The finished place mat is 12½ × 16½ inches.

MATERIALS (for 2 place mats)
Note: Yardages are figured for fabric 45 inches wide.
¼ yard green solid fabric
¼ yard pink solid fabric
¾ yards floral print fabric
1 yard thin quilt batting
pink thread
small piece tracing paper
cardboard

CUTTING LIST
Note: All measurements include a ¼-inch seam allowance.
Trace patterns A and B and transfer them to cardboard for templates (see page 13).

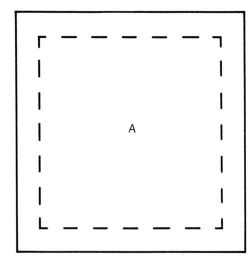

A

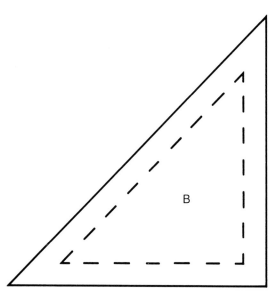

B

Cut the following:

from green solid:
    40 B
from pink solid:
    8 A
    40 B
from floral print:
    2 pieces, each 8½ × 12½ inches
    2 pieces, each 13½ × 17½ for backing
from batting:
    2 pieces, each 12½ × 16½ inches

DIRECTIONS
To make top

1. Refer to Figure 1. With right sides facing, stitch a pink B piece to a green B piece along the diagonal to make a square as shown. Make 40 squares (20 in total for each place mat) in this way.
2. Press seams to one side.
3. Refer to Figure 2. With right sides facing, stitch 2 green-and-pink squares together along one green side edge as shown. Make 20 rectangles (10 in total for each place mat) in this way.
4. Press seams to one side.
5. Refer to Figure 3. With right sides facing, stitch 2 rectangles together along pink edges to make a row as shown. Make 4 rows (2 for each place mat) in this way. These are the side borders.
6. Refer to Figure 4. Next, stitch 3 rectangles together in a row. Then stitch a pink A piece to each end of this row as shown. Make 4 rows (2 for each place mat) in this way. These are the top and bottom border pieces.
7. Press all seams to one side.

Figure 1

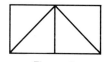

Figure 2

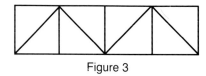

Figure 3

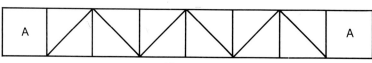

Figure 4

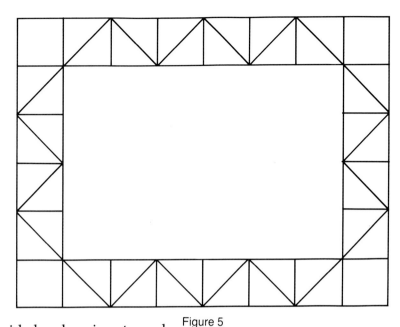

Figure 5

To assemble place mats

See Figure 5.
1. With right sides facing, stitch a side border piece to each short side of the 8½ × 12½ inch floral piece.
2. Press seams to one side.
3. Next, stitch the top and bottom border pieces to the floral piece.
4. Press seams to one side.
5. Repeat for the other place mat.

To quilt

1. With wrong sides facing and batting between, pin the backing, batting and place mat top together.
2. Using pink thread, machine- or hand-quilt ⅛ inch on the inside of the seam lines of all the pink triangles and corner squares. (See page 15 for quilting instructions.)
3. When all quilting is complete, remove the pins and press.

To finish

1. Trim the batting to the same size as the place mat top.
2. Turn the edges of the backing forward ¼ inch and press. Then fold the edges over onto the top of the place mat ¼ inch to make a border all around. Press.
3. Machine-stitch around each side as close to the inside edge as possible.

To make napkins

You will need a yard of fabric to make 4 napkins, each 17 × 17 inches. Cut each square 18 × 18 inches. Turn all raw edges to wrong side ¼ inch and press. Turn another ¼ inch, press and machine- or slip-stitch all around.

83

Flowers and Bows Lap Throw

If you've made new curtains, a bedspread, or even a piece of clothing, chances are you have leftover remnants, or a few inches of the full width of fabrics in different prints or colors. These strips may seem too small to make anything other than a sachet or potholder, but they can be cut into squares of equal size and then joined to make a pretty lap throw. Nothing is easier to make than a small quilt with pieced squares. The trick to making it look good is the selection and combination of fabrics and colors. This pretty pastel floral throw was made from fabrics left over from other home accessories such as curtains and slipcovers, in the same room. It uses 4-inch squares and measures 40 × 48 inches.

MATERIALS

Note: Yardages are figured for fabric 45 inches wide.

A small amount of 8 different fabrics that look good together in the following amounts:
⅛ yard fabric A
⅛ yard fabric B
1½ yards fabric C (includes borders)
¼ yard D
¼ yard E
⅛ yard F
⅛ yard G
⅛ yard H
1½ yards backing fabric
quilt batting 40 × 47 inches

CUTTING LIST

Note: All measurements include a ¼-inch seam allowance.
Trace the square pattern and transfer it to cardboard to
  make a template (see page 13).

Cut the following:

from A:
   6 squares
from B:
   4 squares
from C:
   (Cut borders before cutting squares.)
   2 strips, each 4 × 40½ inches (side borders)
   2 strips, each 4 × 39½ inches (top and bottom borders)
   16 squares
from D:
   18 squares
from E:
   16 squares
from F:
   8 squares
from G:
   8 squares
from H:
   4 squares

F	B	E	H	A	D	C	E
B	E	H	A	D	C	E	G
E	H	A	D	C	E	G	D
H	A	D	C	E	G	D	F
A	D	C	E	G	D	F	C
D	C	E	G	D	F	C	E
C	E	G	D	F	C	E	D
E	G	D	F	C	E	D	C
G	D	F	C	E	D	C	B
D	F	C	E	D	C	B	A

Figure 1

DIRECTIONS

To make rows

Refer to Figure 1.
1. With right sides facing, join an F square and a B square along the side edge. Press seams to one side.
2. With right sides facing, join an E square to the opposite side edge of the B square. Press seams to one side.
3. Continue to join an H square, then an A square, followed by a D square, then a C square, and end Row 1 with an E square.
4. Press seams to one side.
5. Refer to Figure 1 for the color sequence and make 10 rows of 8 squares in this way.

To join rows

Refer to Figure 1.
1. With right sides facing and seam aligned, join the bottom long edge of Row 1 to the top long edge of Row 2. Press seams to one side.
2. Continue to join rows in this way in the sequence shown.

To join borders

1. With right sides facing, join a longer border strip to one side edge of the quilt top.
2. Press seams to one side.
3. Repeat on the opposite side edge of the quilt in the same way.
4. With right sides facing, join one of the remaining shorter border strips to the top edge of the quilt. Press seams to one side.
5. Repeat with the bottom border strip in the same way.

To quilt

1. Cut the backing fabric $42\frac{1}{2} \times 50\frac{1}{2}$ inches.
2. With wrong sides facing and batting between, pin backing, batting, and top together. There will be $1\frac{1}{2}$ inches of extra backing fabric all around.
3. Beginning at the center and working outward in a sunburst pattern, take long, loose, basting stitches through all 3 layers.
4. Using small running stitches, quilt $\frac{1}{4}$ inch on each side of all seam lines, stopping short of the seam allowance all around the outside edge of the quilt.

To finish

1. When all quilting is complete, remove the basting stitches.
2. Trim the batting to the same size as the quilt top.
3. Fold $\frac{1}{4}$ inch of backing fabric forward and press.
4. Bring the remaining backing fabric forward to encase the raw edges of the quilt and create a 1-inch border around the top of the quilt.
5. Press and slip-stitch all around to finish.

Sweet Scent-sations

Pretty patchwork sachets are fun to make and give as gifts or use to scent your dresser drawers, closets, and linens. I used pastel floral prints combined with striped fabric and solid pastels, then edged each pillow sachet with eyelet ruffles. Each sachet is 6 inches square without the 2- or 3-inch ruffle. There are 3 different designs that are quick and easy to make from scraps of fabric. All the designs are made from squares or triangles pieced into squares.

MATERIALS
Small amounts each of a matching floral print, striped fabric, and pastel
6½ × 6½-inch backing fabric for each sachet
1 yard 2- or 3-inch-wide pregathered eyelet ruffle for each sachet
1 yard piping if desired for each sachet
potpourri or stuffing for each pillow
tracing paper
cardboard

CUTTING LIST
Note: All measurements include a ¼-inch seam allowance.
Trace patterns A and B and transfer them to cardboard to make templates (see page 13).

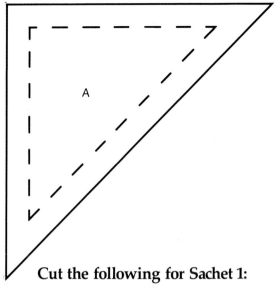

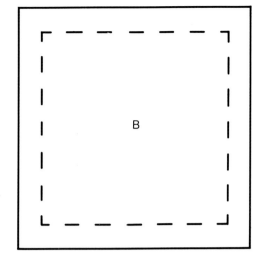

A

B

Cut the following for Sachet 1:

from floral print:
    4 A
    1 B
from stripe:
    4 B
from pastel solid:
    4 A

Cut the following for Sachet 2:

from floral print:
    4 A
    4 B
from stripe:
    4 A
    1 B

Cut the following for Sachet 3:

from floral print:
    9 A
from stripe:
    9 A

DIRECTIONS
To assemble Sachet 1

Note: This is a Pinwheel design. Refer to Figure 1 for placement of squares.

1. With right sides facing, join a floral A piece to a pastel solid A piece along the diagonal to make a square.

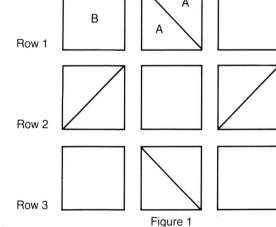

Figure 1

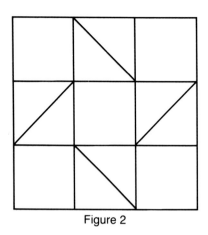

Figure 2

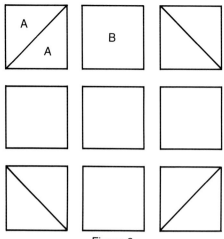

Figure 3

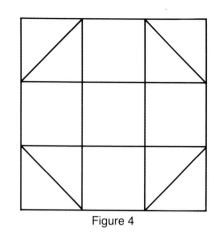

Figure 4

2. Press seams to one side. Make 4 squares in this way.
3. With right sides facing, join a pieced square to a striped B square along one side edge. Press seams to one side.
4. Next, join another striped B square to the opposite side of the pieced square to complete Row 1.
5. To make Row 2, join a pieced square to each side of a floral B square in the same way.
6. To make Row 3, join a striped B square to each side edge of a pieced square.
7. With right sides facing and seams aligned, join all 3 rows to complete the sachet top as shown in Figure 2.

To assemble Sachet 2

Refer to Figure 3.
1. With right sides facing, join a floral A piece to a striped A piece along the diagonal to make a square.
2. Press seams to one side. Make 4 squares in this way.
3. With right sides facing, join a pieced square to a floral B square along one side edge.
4. Next, join another pieced square to the opposite side of the floral B square to complete Row 1 as shown. Press seams to one side.
5. To make Row 2, join a floral B square to each side edge of a striped B square as shown. Press seams to one side.
6. To make Row 3, join a pieced square to each side edge of a floral B square as shown. Press seams to one side.
7. With right sides facing and seams aligned, join all 3 rows. Press seams to one side to complete the sachet top as shown in Figure 4.

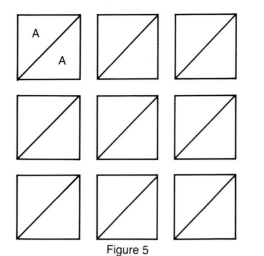

Figure 5

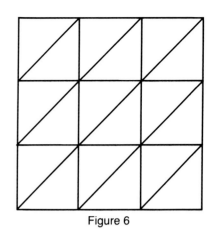

Figure 6

To assemble Sachet 3

Note: When piecing stripes and floral triangles be sure the stripes are all positioned in the same direction. Refer to Figure 5.

1. With right sides facing, join a striped A piece to a floral A piece along the diagonal to make a square.
2. Press seams to one side. Make 9 squares in this way.
3. Arrange the squares in 3 rows of 3 squares each with the floral triangles on the left and stripes on the right.
4. With right sides facing, join the squares to make rows.
5. With right sides facing and seams aligned, join all 3 rows, as shown in Figure 6.

To finish all sachets

1. With right sides facing and raw edges aligned, stitch the piping around the patchwork top of each sachet.
2. Next, with right sides facing and raw edges aligned, pin the eyelet ruffle around the sachet top.
3. Using the piping stitches as a guide, join the eyelet ruffle to the sachet top.
4. With right sides facing and the ruffle between, pin the backing fabric to the sachet top.
5. Stitch around 3 sides and 4 corners, leaving 3 inches open for turning and stuffing.
6. Clip the corners and trim the seam allowance. Turn right side out and press if needed.
7. Fill each sachet with your favorite potpourri mixture or fiberfill stuffing to which you have added a drop or two of perfume.
8. Turn the raw edges of the opening to the inside and slip-stitch closed.

Floral Table Runner

The Bear Claw and Churn Dash patterns are combined here in two blocks divided by lattice strips and borders to make a table runner. My daughter, Robby, had pieced the blocks to make two pillows, but when we arranged them on a table they looked so good, we joined them for the runner. However, as you can see, each block would make a nice pillow, and if you wanted to continue making blocks, this pattern would make a very pretty quilt as well. The floral print and solids in apricot and aqua give the table a fresh, springtime look that can be enjoyed all year long. The finished size is 20½ × 39 inches. To make the runner longer, simply add another block at each end. To make it wider, add another border or make the border wider than the given measurement.

MATERIALS

Note: Yardages are figured for fabric 45 inches wide.
½ yard off-white solid fabric
½ yard aqua green solid fabric
1¼ yards floral fabric (includes backing)
thin quilt batting 20½ × 39½ inches
tracing paper
cardboard

CUTTING LIST

Note: All measurements include a ¼-inch seam allowance.
Trace patterns A, B, C, D, E, F, G, and H and transfer them
to cardboard for templates (see page 13).

Cut the following

from off-white solid:

16 B

4 A

4 D

4 E

4 F

4 G

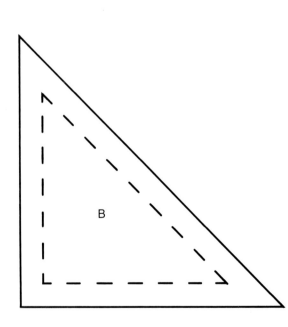

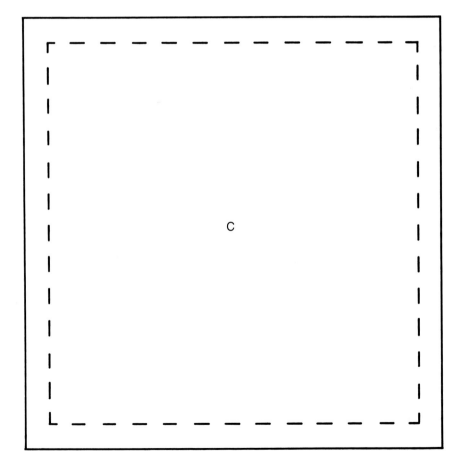

D and F

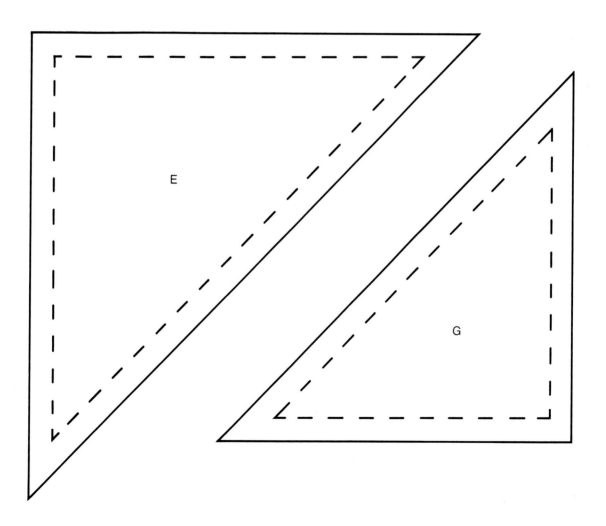

E

G

H

from floral print:
   2 strips, each 2½ × 39½ inches
   3 strips, each 2½ × 16½ inches
   1 piece for backing, 21 × 40 inches
    1 A
   16 B
    4 C
    4 E
    4 F
    1 H
from aqua green solid:
   4 strips, each 1¾ × 14½ inches (top and bottom lattice
     strips)
   4 strips, each 1¾ × 16½ inches (side lattice strips)

DIRECTIONS
To make Bear Claw block

1. Refer to Figure 1. With right sides facing, join a floral B piece to an off-white B piece along the diagonal to make a square as shown.

2. Press seams to one side. Make 4 squares in this way.

3. Refer to Figure 2. With right sides facing, join two of the squares made in Figure 1 to make a horizontal row. Press seams to one side.

4. Refer to Figure 3. With right sides facing, join an off-white A square and 2 of the pieced squares made in Figure 1 as shown to make a vertical row. Press seams to one side.

5. Refer to Figure 4. With right sides facing, join the row made in Figure 2 to the top edge of a floral C piece. Press seams to one side.

6. Refer to Figure 5. Join the row made in Figure 3 to the left side of the floral C piece to make a section as shown.

7. Press seams to one side. Make 4 sections in this way.

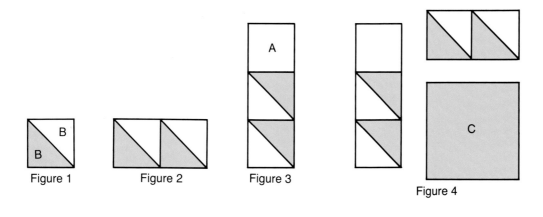

Figure 1   Figure 2   Figure 3   Figure 4

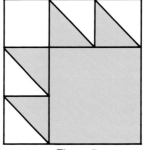

Figure 5

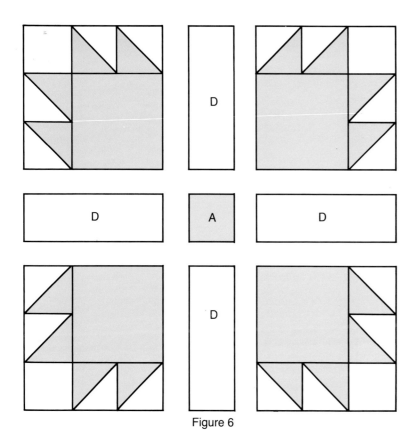

Figure 6

To assemble sections

Refer to Figure 6.

1. With right sides facing, join an off-white D piece to the right side edge of a pieced section. Press seams to one side.

2. With right sides facing, join another pieced section to the opposite side edge of the off-white D piece in the same way to make the top row.

3. Press seams to one side. Make another section in the same way, only in reverse, as shown, to make the bottom row.

4. To make the divider strip, stitch the short end of an off-white D piece to the floral A piece and then to the short end of another off-white D piece. Press seams to one side.

5. With right sides facing, stitch the bottom edge of the top row to the top edge of the divider strip. Then stitch the bottom edge of the divider strip to the top edge of the bottom row to make the Bear Claw block.

6. Press seams to one side.

To make Churn Dash block

1. Refer to Figure 7. With right sides facing, join an off-white E piece to a floral E piece along the diagonal to make a square as shown.

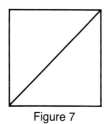

Figure 7

2. Press seams to one side. Make 4 squares in this way.
3. Refer to Figure 8. With right sides facing, join an off-white F piece to a floral F piece along one long edge as shown.
4. Press seams to one side. Make 4 pieces in this way.
5. Refer to Figure 9. With right sides facing, join the diagonal edge of an off-white G piece to one side edge of the floral H square. Repeat with the remaining 3 off-white G pieces to make a larger square as shown.
6. Press seams to one side.

To assemble

Refer to Figure 10.
1. Arrange all the sections into 3 rows as shown.
2. With right sides facing, join the top 3 pieces to make the top row. Next, join the middle 3 pieces to make the middle row and then join the bottom 3 pieces to make the bottom row.
3. Press seams to one side.
4. With right sides facing, join the bottom edge of the top row across the top edge of the middle row. Then join the bottom row in the same way.
5. Press seams to one side.

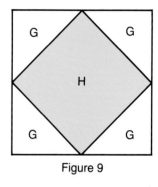

Figure 8

Figure 9

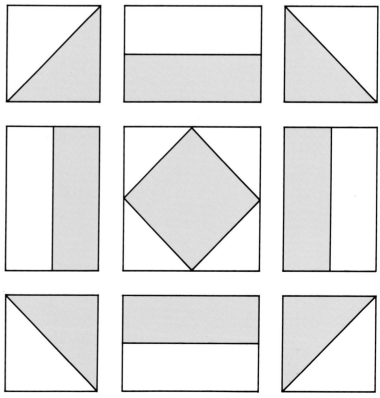

Figure 10

To join lattice strips

Refer to Figure 11.

1. With right sides facing, stitch one of the shorter aqua green border strips across the top edge of each block. Press seams to one side.

2. With right sides facing, join the other 2 shorter aqua green border strips to the bottom edges of the blocks in the same way.

3. With right sides facing, stitch a remaining aqua green border strip to each side edge of each block.

4. Press seams to one side.

5. With right sides facing, join a short floral lattice strip to the one side edge of the Bear Claw block. Press seams to one side.

6. With right sides facing, join the Churn Dash block to the opposite side of the floral strip in the same way.

To join borders

Refer to Figure 11.

1. With right sides facing, join a short floral lattice strip to the remaining side edge of the Bear Claw block.

2. Press seams to one side.

3. Next, join the remaining short floral border strip to the remaining side edge of the Churn Dash block in the same way.

4. With right sides facing, join the long floral borders to the top and bottom edges of the runner in the same way.

To quilt

1. With wrong sides facing and the batting between, pin the backing, batting, and pieced top together.

2. Beginning in the center and working outward in a sunburst pattern, take long, loose basting stitches through all 3 layers.

3. Using small running stitches, quilt ¼ inch on each side of all seam lines, stopping short of the seam allowance around the outside edge.

To finish

1. When all quilting is complete, remove the basting stitches.

2. Trim the batting ¼ inch smaller than the top all around.

3. Turn the raw edges of the backing and the pieced top to the inside ¼ inch and press.

4. Machine-stitch all around to finish.

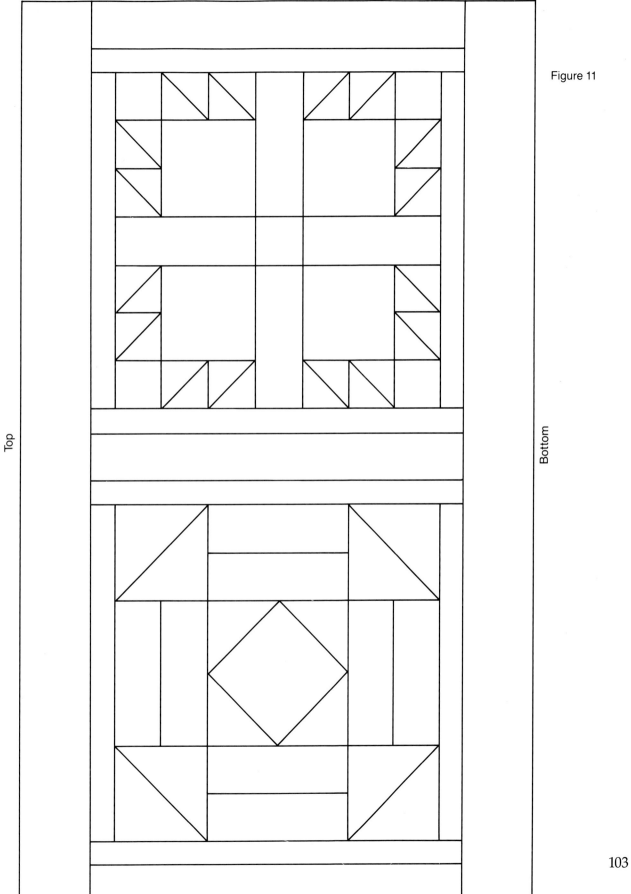

Top

Bottom

Figure 11

103

Pillow Passion

Little throw pillows make delightful accents on a sofa or bed. These simple patchwork patterns are easy to stitch up in an afternoon and the hand-quilting adds an interesting dimension. Make up your own quilting patterns of lines, diamonds, swirls or leaves and do as much or as little as desired. Each pillow is 12 × 12 inches. You can stuff the pillows with fiberfill or you can use standard-size pillow forms.

MATERIALS (for both pillows)
¼ yard muslin or white solid fabric
½ yard peach calico
2 pieces quilt batting, each 12 × 12 inches
3 yards cording (1½ yards for each pillow)
   stuffing or 12 × 12-inch pillow form
tracing paper
cardboard
quilt marking pen

CUTTING LIST
Note: All measurements include a ¼-inch seam allowance.
Trace patterns A, B, C, D, E, F, and G and transfer them to cardboard for templates (see page 13).

A

B

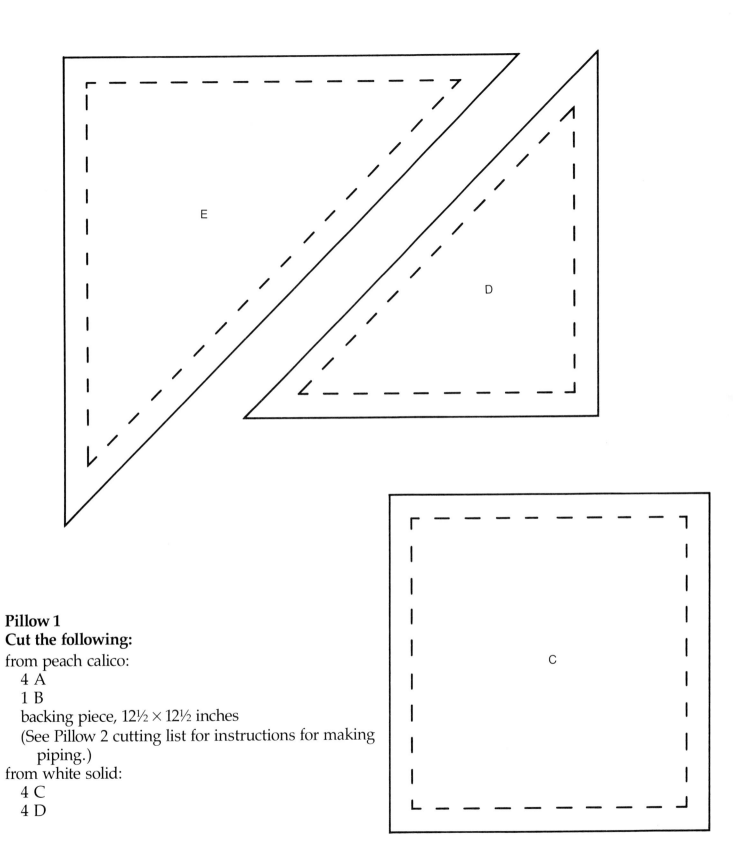

E

D

C

Pillow 1
Cut the following:
from peach calico:
   4 A
   1 B
   backing piece, 12½ × 12½ inches
   (See Pillow 2 cutting list for instructions for making
     piping.)
from white solid:
   4 C
   4 D

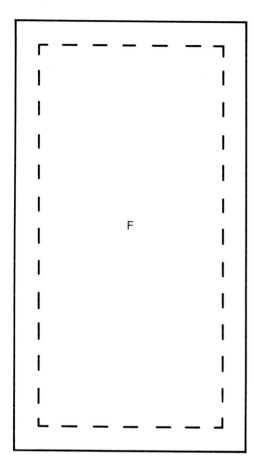

Pillow 2
Cut the following:
from peach calico:
    4 E
    4 F
    backing piece, 12½ × 12½ inches
    Cut strips 1½ inches wide and piece them together to
        make 2 strips, each 1½ × 49 inches, for the piping of
        both pillows.
from white solid:
    4 E
    4 F
    1 G

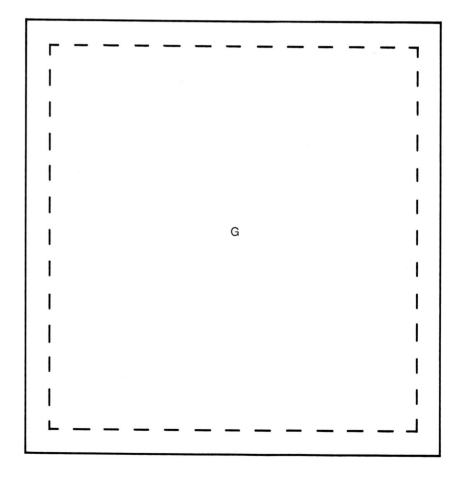

DIRECTIONS

Pillow 1

To make pillow top

1. Refer to Figure 1. With right sides facing, stitch the diagonal edge of a white D piece to each side edge of the peach B piece to make a larger square.
2. Press seams to one side.
3. Refer to Figure 2 and, with right sides facing and edges aligned, stitch the long edge of a peach A piece to one side edge of this square as shown. Repeat with another A piece on the opposite side of the square to make the center section of the pillow top.
4. Refer to Figure 3. With right sides facing, stitch a white C piece to each short end of another peach A piece to make a strip.
5. Repeat with the remaining 2 white C pieces and peach A piece.
6. Refer to Figure 4. With right sides facing, join one of these strips to the top edge of the center section and one strip to the bottom edge of the center section to make the pillow top as shown.
7. Press seams to one side.

To finish

1. Cover the cording with a 49-inch-long peach fabric strip to make piping. Using a zipper foot on your sewing machine, stitch close to cording to encase it inside the fabric with raw edges aligned.
2. Stitch the piping to the right side of the pillow top.
3. With right sides facing and the piping between, pin the pillow top and the backing piece together.
4. Using the piping stitches as a guide, stitch around 3 sides and 4 corners.
5. Trim the seam allowance, clip the corners, and turn fabric right side out. Press.
6. Stuff to desired fullness or insert a pillow form.
7. Turn the raw edges of the opening to the inside and press. Slip-stitch the opening closed.

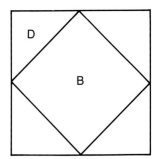

Figure 1

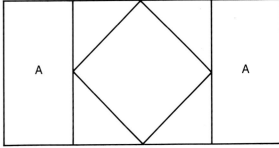

Figure 2

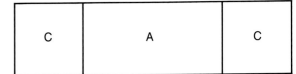

Figure 3

Pillow 1

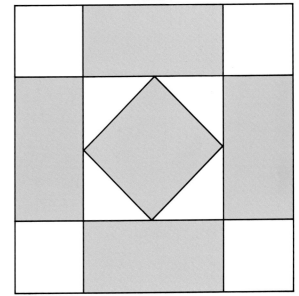

Figure 4

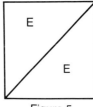

Figure 5

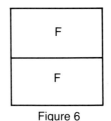

Figure 6

Pillow 2
To make pillow top
1. Refer to Figure 5. With right sides facing, join a peach E piece to a white E piece along the diagonal edge to make a square. Make 4 squares in this way. These are the corner squares.
2. Press seams to one side.
3. Refer to Figure 6. With right sides facing, stitch a peach F to a white F piece along the long edge to make a square. Make 4 squares in this way. These are the side squares.
4. Press seams to one side.
5. Refer to Figure 7 and stitch a corner square to a side square, then that rectangle to another corner square to make the top row of the pillow top.
6. Next, stitch a side square to each side of the white G piece to make the middle row of the pillow top.
7. Repeat step 5 for the bottom row of the pillow top.
8. Press seams to one side.
9. Refer to Figure 7. With right sides facing, join rows to finish the top of the pillow.

To finish
Using the remaining 49-inch-long peach fabric strip, finish in the same way as Pillow 1 (see page 109).

Pillow 2

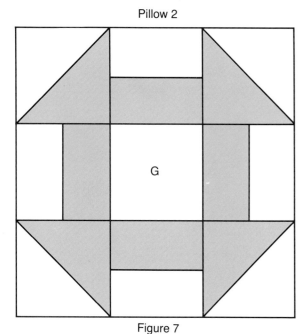

Figure 7

Victorian Christmas Stocking

Get out all your elegant fabric scraps to make an old-fashioned Christmas stocking. Angela Thomas combined floral and paisley prints in rich shades of purple, green, lavender, and rose to give this project a distinctly Victorian flavor. The lining and cuff are made from pink satin moire and edged with white fringe. The stocking measures approximately 17 inches from cuff to toe.

MATERIALS

Note: Yardages are figured for fabric 45 inches wide.
scraps of different fabrics
¼ yard pink moire for lining and cuff
¼ yard thin quilt batting
14 inches white fringe
tracing paper

DIRECTIONS

Note: All measurements include a ¼-inch seam allowance. You can make the patchwork fabric in either of two ways. If you want to copy the stocking shown here, enlarge the pattern (see page 12) and transfer each piece to cardboard to make a template (see page 13). Or you can simply stitch

together a variety of sizes and shapes of scraps to create a piece of fabric approximately 6 × 18 inches for the front of the stocking. The backing can be solid or you can make another patchwork piece for the back as well. If you use the pattern pieces provided here, add a ¼-inch seam allowance to each when cutting it out.

To make patchwork

Refer to Figure 1 for piecing the fabric.

1. With right sides facing, join piece 1 to piece 2 along the edge as shown. Press seams to one side.
2. With right sides facing, join piece 3 to the bottom edge of this unit as shown. Press seams to one side.
3. Next, join piece 4 to one long edge as shown, followed by piece 5. Press seams to one side.
4. Next, join piece 6, followed by piece 7, then piece 8 in the same way.
5. With right sides facing, join piece 9 to piece 10 along one edge. Press seams to one side.
6. With right sides facing, join this to the raw edge of 7 and 8 as shown. Press seams to one side.
7. Join pieces 11 and 12 in the same way, then join to the larger pieced section.
8. Join piece 13 to the raw edge of the pieced stocking.
9. With right sides facing, join pieces 14, 15, 16, and 17.

To make stocking

1. Enlarge the stocking pattern (see page 12), cut it out, and pin it to the backing fabric.
2. Cut out 1 backing piece allowing for ¼-inch seam allowance all around.
3. Use the pattern piece to cut 2 lining pieces with ¼-inch seam allowance added.
4. If you have simply stitched several odd pieces of fabric together to create a patchwork piece rather than using the pattern pieces provided, use the stocking pattern to cut this shape from your patchwork, making sure to add the ¼-inch seam allowance all around.
5. Next, use the pattern (without seam allowance) to cut 2 stocking shapes from the thin quilt batting.
6. With right sides facing, pin the backing to the patchwork top piece and, starting at the back top edge of the stocking,

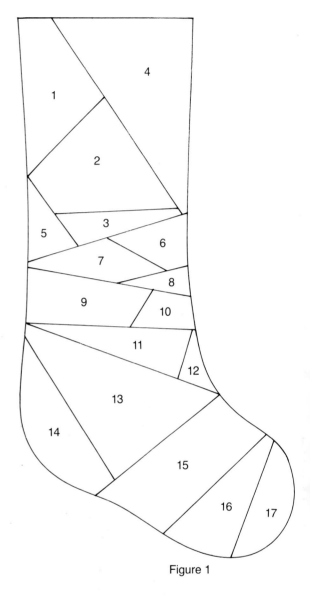

Figure 1

stitch around to the opposite side edge, leaving the top open all around.

7. Clip into the seam allowance at all curves. Trim seam allowance as close to the stitches as possible. Turn right side out and press.

8. With right sides facing, pin together a quilt batting piece, a lining piece, then another lining piece, followed by the other batting piece, leaving the top edge open.

9. Stitch around as you did for the outer stocking, just catching the edge of the batting in seam, but do not turn right side out.

To finish

1. Insert the lining and quilt batting piece into the stocking and push the toe down in place all around, aligning the side seams as you do this.

2. Fold the top edges of the lining and the stocking to the inside between both layers of fabric and press.

3. Pin the raw edge of the fringe between the lining and the outside of the stocking around the top edge and pin.

4. Slip-stitch or machine-stitch all around the top edge. Tack the lining and the stocking together at the toe and the heel in the seam line if needed.

5. Fold the top edge of the stocking to the outside to create a 2½-inch cuff. Add a decorative ring or make a loop with embroidery floss at the back seam line for hanging if desired.

Sail Away

This pattern is often called Sunshine and Shadow and is a popular Amish design. Half of each square is dark, the other half is light. When you combine light and dark colors you'll achieve a dramatic effect. By using a blue background and blue stripes, the triangles look like sailboats. Like many piecing projects, it appears to be more difficult than it is. The secret is the strip-piecing sewing method. This crib quilt is 36 × 43 inches and makes a wonderful gift for the new baby.

MATERIALS

Note: All yardage is figured for fabric 45 inches wide.
⅛ yard mint green solid fabric
⅛ yard lavender solid fabric
¼ yard white solid fabric
1 yard aqua solid fabric
1¾ yards navy blue solid fabric (includes backing)
quilt batting 36 × 43 inches
tracing paper
cardboard
quilt marking pen

CUTTING LIST

Note: All measurements include a ¼-inch seam allowance. Trace the pattern, which is half the size needed, then turn the tracing over and trace again to complete the full-size A pattern. Transfer it to cardboard for a template (see page 13).

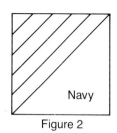

Navy

Figure 2

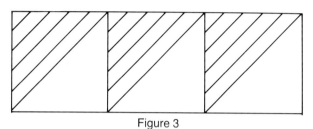

Figure 3

To make a block

Refer to Figure 2.

1. With right sides facing, join a triangle made from strips to a navy triangle along the diagonal to make a block.
2. Press seams to one side. Make 12 blocks in this way.

To make a row

Refer to Figure 3.

1. With right sides facing, join the side edge of one block to the side edge of another block.
2. Press seams to one side.
3. Next, continue by adding another block to make a row of 3 blocks. Make 4 rows in this way.

To join rows

Refer to Figure 4.

1. With right sides facing, join the top edge of one row to the bottom edge of another row.
2. Press seams to one side.
3. Continue to join all 4 rows in this way.

To join borders

Refer to Figure 4.

1. With right sides facing, join a shorter aqua border strip to the top edge of the joined rows.
2. Press seams to one side.
3. Repeat on the bottom edge of the quilt top.
4. Next, join the longer aqua border strips to the side edges of the quilt top in the same way.

To quilt

1. Beginning at the top corner edge of the aqua border, mark off a 1-inch grid on the diagonal across the borders only.
2. With wrong sides facing and batting between, pin the backing fabric, batting, and quilt top together.
3. Beginning at the center and working outward in a sunburst pattern, take long, loose basting stitches through all 3 layers.
4. Using small running stitches, quilt along all premarked lines, stopping short of the seam allowance all around the outside edge of the quilt.
5. When all quilting is complete, remove the basting stitches.

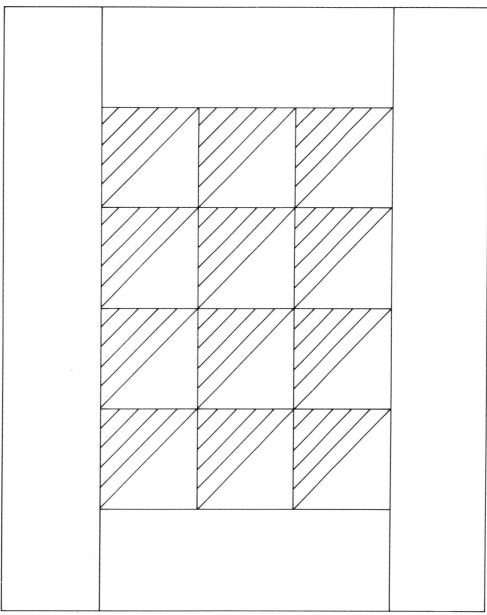

Figure 4

To finish

1. Trim the batting ½ inch smaller than the quilt top all around.

2. Trim the backing to 1 inch larger than the quilt top all around.

3. Turn the raw edges of the backing to the inside ¼ inch all around and press.

4. Next, turn the backing over ½ inch onto the quilt top and pin all around to create a ½-inch navy border around the quilt.

5. Slip-stitch or machine-stitch all around to finish.

119

Wildflower Medley

*Measuring 12 inches tall, this feed sack-shaped
tote bag is the perfect size to carry anything
from everyday necessities to picnic fare. Nancy
Moore took a break from her business of
custom-making boat cushions and sails to
create a cheerful carryall. This project shows
how quilting a pretty piece of fabric can
enhance any sewing project. Nancy used a
piece of 1-inch-wide webbing (sold in notions
stores) for the strap and brass grommets to
attach the rope drawstring. A set of grommets
and the tool to apply them can be found at
most hardware and home center stores as well
as some five and dimes. The bag is 12 inches
high and 10 inches wide.*

MATERIALS
Note: Yardages are figured for fabric 45 inches wide.
½ yard of floral print fabric
½ yard solid fabric for lining
½ yard thin quilting
1 yard piping
1 yard 1-inch-wide webbing for strap
1 yard cording for drawstring
package of grommets
tracing paper
quilt marking pen

CUTTING LIST

Note: All measurements include a ¼-inch seam allowance. Trace the pattern, which represents half the bottom of the bag, then turn the tracing over and trace again to complete the full-size pattern. Cut out the pattern and use it to cut the fabric. Or you can place the pattern shown here on the fold of the fabric.

Cut the following:

from floral print:
    1 piece, 14½ × 27½ inches
    1 pattern piece
from solid:
    1 piece, 14½ × 27½ inches for lining
    1 pattern piece
from quilt batting:
    1 piece, 14½ × 27½ inches
    1 pattern piece

DIRECTIONS
To quilt fabric

1. Using the quilt marking pen and a ruler, mark off diagonal lines 4 inches apart across the rectangular floral fabric in each direction to make a diamond grid.
2. With wrong sides facing and the batting between, pin the rectangular lining, batting, and floral pieces together.
3. Using a loose stitch setting on your machine (6–7 stitches per inch), quilt along all marked lines through all 3 layers of fabric to quilt the body of the bag.
4. Repeat steps 1–3 with the oval floral fabric piece, batting, and lining to quilt the bottom of the bag.

To assemble bag

1. With right sides facing and raw edges aligned, join the piping to one long raw edge of the quilted body.
2. Measure down 2¼ inches from the opposite long edge of the floral fabric and, beginning at one short edge, mark every 2½ inches for grommet placement. Insert grommets according to package directions or make buttonholes for drawstring cord.
3. With right sides facing, fold the quilted floral fabric in half, aligning short edges, and stitch together along one edge to create a tube.

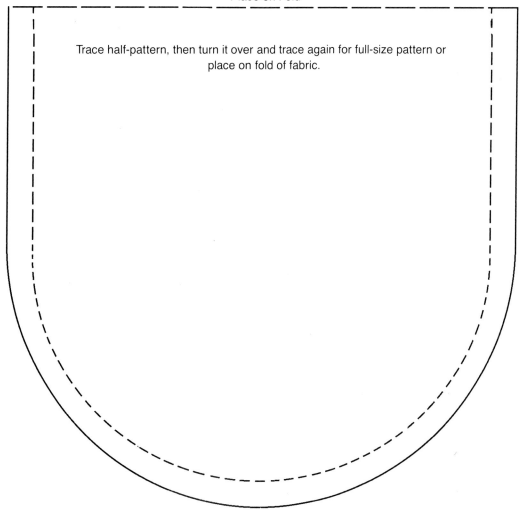

Place on Fold

Trace half-pattern, then turn it over and trace again for full-size pattern or place on fold of fabric.

4. Turn the grommet edge of the body under ¼ inch and press. Fold this edge 1½ inches to the inside and stitch across the bag. Stitch another line ⅛ inch from the top, folded edge.

5. With right sides facing and piping between, pin the bottom piece to the raw edge of the body all around. Stitch together and turn right side out.

To finish

1. Weave the cording through the grommets and tie a knot on each end.

2. Fold the raw ends of the webbing strap under and pin in position 3 inches down on each side of the bag.

3. Stitch across the top and bottom edges to secure the straps.

Casual Country Pillow

This pillow is made with the same printed fabric in different colors. The faded barn red, white, and Shaker blue colors give a country feeling to the traditional red, white, and blue patriotic theme. Make any sofa or chair look inviting with this tailored, patchwork pillow that measures 15 × 15 inches.

MATERIALS
Note: Yardages are figured for fabric 45 inches wide.
red print fabric 8 × 10 inches
½ yard blue print fabric (includes backing)
off-white print fabric 20 × 20 inches
thin quilt batting 15 × 15 inches
12-inch blue or off-white zipper (optional)
stuffing
tracing paper
cardboard

CUTTING LIST
Note: All measurements include a ¼-inch seam allowance.
Trace patterns A, B, C, and D and transfer them to cardboard for templates (see page 13).

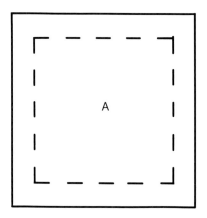

Cut the following:
from off-white print:
    20 A
      4 C
      1 D
from blue print:
    1 piece, 15½ × 15½ inches for backing
    16 A
    2 strips, each 1¼ × 14 inches
    2 strips, each 1¼ × 15½ inches
from red print:
    4 B

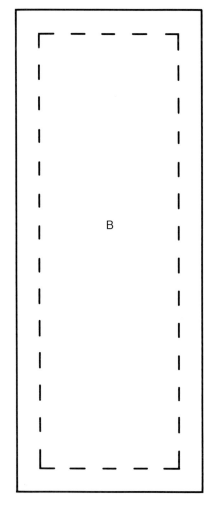

C

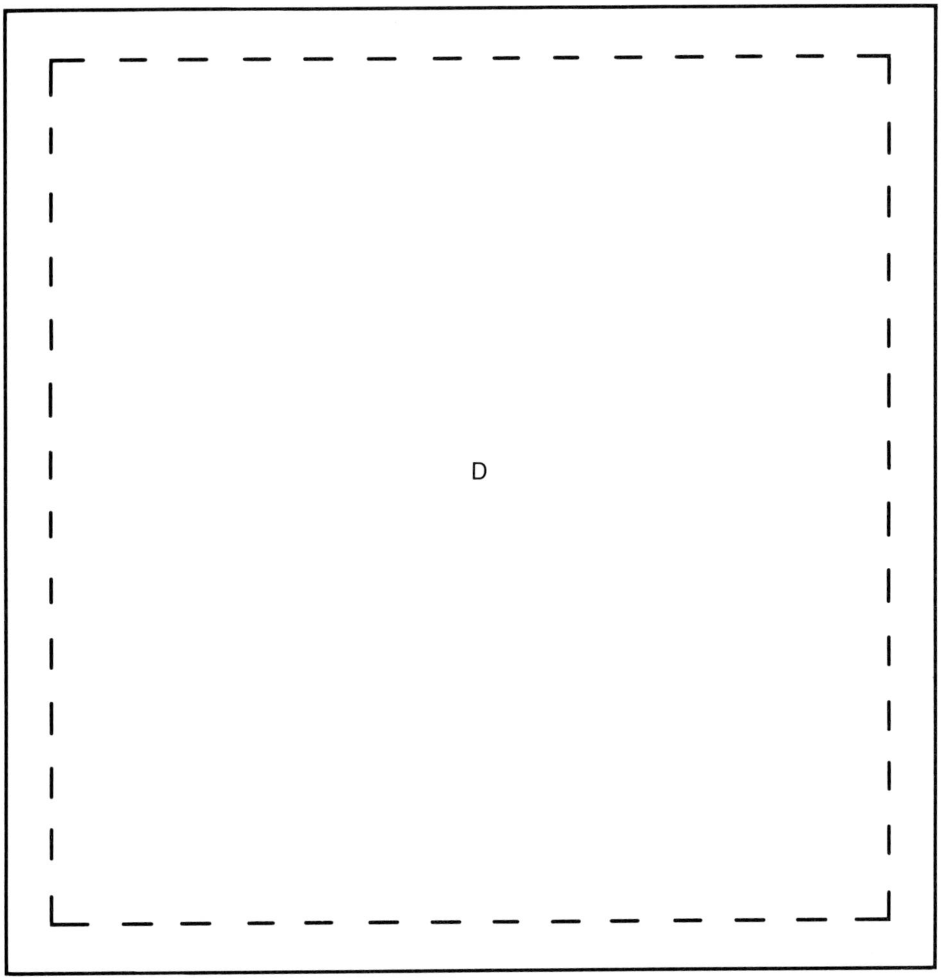

D

DIRECTIONS
To make corner units

Refer to Figure 1.

1. With right sides facing, join a white A piece and a blue A piece along one side edge.

2. Press seams to one side.

3. With right sides facing, join another white A piece to the opposite side edge of the blue A piece to make a row of 3 squares. Press seams and repeat to make Rows 1 and 3.

4. With right sides facing, join a blue A square to a white A square followed by another blue A square to make the middle row. Press seams to one side.

5. Refer to Figure 2. With right sides facing and seams aligned, join all 3 rows along the long edges. Press seams to one side. Make 4 blocks in this way.

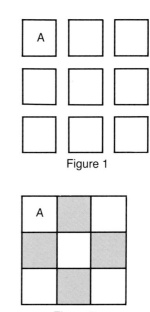

Figure 1

Figure 2

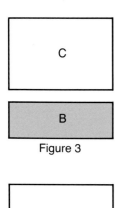

C

Figure 3

B

C

Figure 4

B

To make rectangular units

Refer to Figure 3.

1. With right sides facing, join a white C piece to a red B piece along one long edge.

2. Open seams and press. Make 4 in this way. See Figure 4.

To assemble pillow top

Refer to Figure 5.

1. With right sides facing, join a corner unit to a pieced rectangular unit as shown. Press seams to one side.

2. Next, join another corner unit in the same way to complete Row 1.

3. With right sides facing, join a rectangular unit to the D square along one side edge as shown. Press seams to one side.

4. Next join another rectangular unit to the opposite side of the square to complete Row 2.

5. With the center rectangular unit in the reverse position, make Row 3 as you did Row 1.

6. Refer to Figure 6. With right sides facing and seams aligned, join all 3 rows. Press seams to one side.

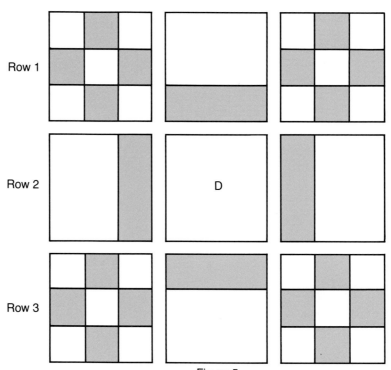

Row 1

Row 2

Row 3

D

Figure 5

To add borders
1. Join the shorter blue strips to the top and bottom.
2. Press.
3. Join the remaining blue strips to each side edge and press.

To quilt
1. Pin the pillow top to the quilt batting.
2. Using small running stitches, quilt ¼ inch on each side of all seam lines.

To finish
1. When all quilting is complete, remove the pins.
2. With right sides facing, pin the backing piece to the quilt top.
3. Stitch around 4 corners and 3 sides, leaving a 12-inch opening on one side.
4. Clip the corners and trim the seam allowance all around.
5. Turn the pillow right side out and stuff.
6. Turn the raw edges to the inside and press. You can insert a zipper as directed on the package or slip-stitch the opening closed.

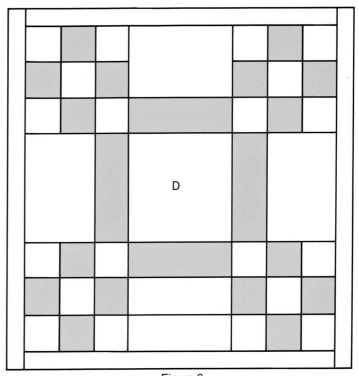

Figure 6

Petal Pale Pillows

A traditional pattern such as the Log Cabin, which is made by joining strips of fabric, is always attractive. Maggie Detmer makes this design seem fresh and new by combining petal soft solid colors for bedroom pillows that look as delicate as a cloud. Each pillow measures 14 × 14 inches.

There is no need to cut small pieces of fabric to make these designs. The ease of these projects comes from the fact that you simply start with a square and add strips of equal width, then cut away the excess fabric from each strip as it is added to make the square ever larger.

MATERIALS (for both pillows)
Note: Yardages are figured for fabric 45 inches wide.
strips of solid fabrics, each 1½ inches wide and in the following lengths and colors: gray (A) (62 inches), slate green (B) (40 inches), tan (C) (34 inches), beige (D) (80 inches), pale peach (E) (41 inches), pale rose (F) (42 inches), pale lavender (G) (60 inches), pale green (H) (50 inches), pale pink (I) (35 inches) and, only for Pillow 2, ecru (J) (22 inches)
½ yard backing fabric
3¼ yards gray piping
stuffing or 2 14 × 14-inch pillow forms

Pillow 1

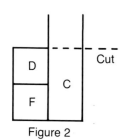

Figure 1

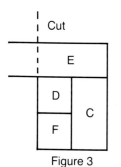

Figure 2

Figure 3

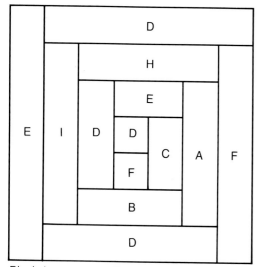

Block 1   Figure 4

CUTTING LIST

Note: All measurements include a ¼-inch seam allowance.

Pillow 1
Cut the following:

from gray (A):
   1 square, 1½ × 1½ inches
from slate green (B):
   1 square, 1½ × 1½ inches
from tan (C):
   1 square, 1½ × 1½ inches
from beige (D):
   2 squares, each 1½ × 1½ inches
from pale peach (E):
   2 squares, each 1½ × 1½ inches
from pale rose (F):
   1 square, 1½ × 1½ inches

Pillow 2
Cut the following:

from gray (A):
   1 square, 1½ × 1½ inches
from slate green (B):
   1 square, 1½ × 1½ inches

DIRECTIONS
Pillow 1
To make Block 1

1. Refer to Figure 1. With right sides facing, join a beige (D) square to a pale rose (F) square along one edge.
2. Press seams to one side.
3. Next, refer to Figure 2 and, with right sides facing join a tan (C) strip along one long edge and cut away excess C fabric. Press seams to one side.
4. Refer to Figure 3 and join a pale peach (E) strip to the top edge of this unit. Cut away excess E fabric as shown. Press seams to one side.
5. Refer to Figure 4 and continue to add strips in color sequence as indicated.

To make Block 2

Refer to Figure 5.
1. With right sides facing, join a slate green (B) square to a

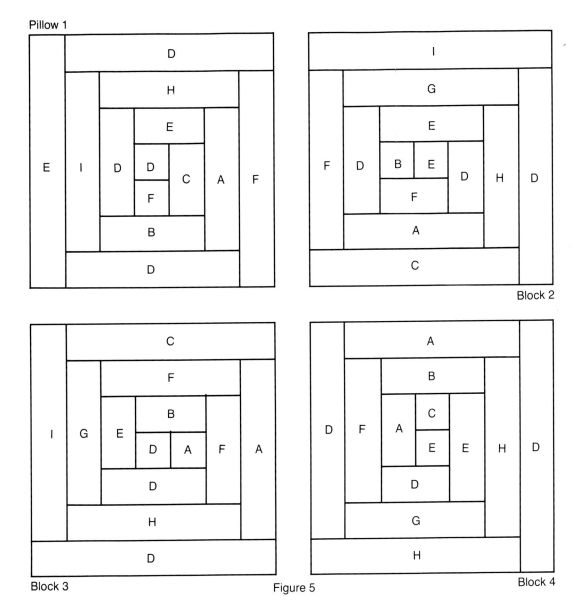

Pillow 1

Block 2

Key
A Gray
B Slate Green
C Tan
D Beige
E Pale Peach
F Pale Rose
G Pale Lavender
H Pale Green
I Pale Pink
   Piping: Gray

Block 3

Figure 5

Block 4

pale peach (E) square along one side. Press seams to one side.

2. Next, add a pale rose (F) strip to one long edge of this unit in the same way. Cut away excess F fabric. Press seams to one side.

3. Continue to add strips in the same way and in the color sequence indicated.

4. Press seams to one side.

To make Block 3

Refer to Figure 5.

1. With right sides facing, join a beige (D) square to a gray (A) square along one side edge. Press seams to one side.

Pillow 2

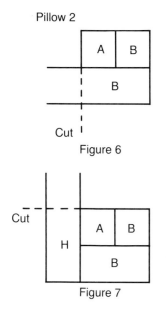

Figure 6

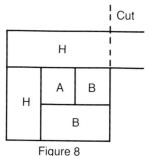

Figure 7

Figure 8

2. Next, join a slate green (B) strip to one long edge of this unit and cut away excess B fabric as before. Press seams to one side.
3. Continue to add strips in this way in the color sequence indicated. Press seams to one side.

To make Block 4

Refer to Figure 5.
1. With right sides facing, join a tan (C) square to a pale peach (E) square along one edge. Press seams to one side.
2. Next, join a gray (A) strip to one long edge as before and cut away excess A fabric.
3. Press seams to one side.
4. Continue to add strips in this way in the color sequence indicated.

To join blocks

Refer to Figure 5.
1. With right sides facing, join Block 1 and Block 2 along the right side edge as shown.
2. Press seams to one side.
3. With right sides facing, join Block 3 and Block 4 in the same way.
4. With right sides facing and seams aligned, join the 2 rows to complete the pillow top. Press seams to one side.

To finish

1. With right sides facing and raw edges aligned, stitch the piping around the top edge of the pillow.
2. Cut the backing to fit the pillow top. With right sides facing and the piping between, pin the backing to the pillow top.
3. Using the piping stitches as a guide, stitch around 4 corners and 3 sides, leaving 8 inches open on one side for turning.
4. Clip the corners and trim the seam allowance. Turn right side out and press. Stuff to desired fullness.
5. Turn raw edges to the inside, press, and slip-stitch closed.

Pillow 2
To make pillow top

1. Refer to Figure 6. With right sides facing, join the gray (A) square to the slate green (B) square along one edge.

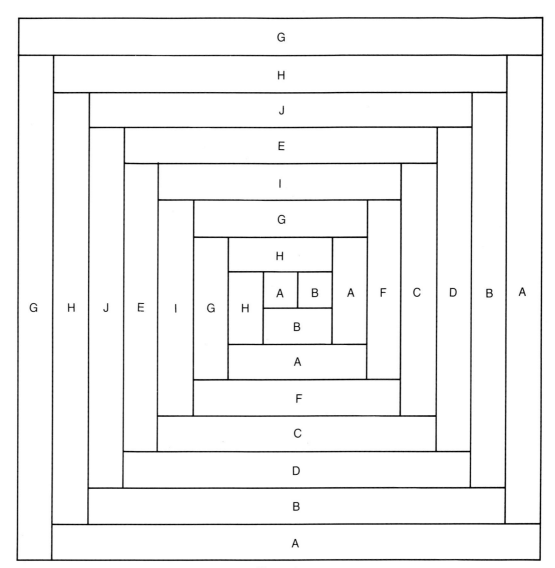

Key
A Gray
B Slate Green
C Tan
D Beige
E Pale Peach
F Pale Rose
G Pale Lavender
H Pale Green
I Pale Pink
J Ecru

Piping: Gray

Figure 9

2. Press seams to one side.

3. Next, join a slate green (B) strip to one long edge of this unit as shown. Cut away excess B fabric and press seams to one side.

4. Refer to Figure 7 and join a pale green (H) strip to the left side edge of this unit. Cut away excess H fabric as shown and press seams to one side.

5. Refer to Figure 8 and join a pale green (H) strip to the top long edge of this unit. Cut away excess H fabric as before and press seams to one side.

6. Refer to Figure 9 and continue to add strips in this way, in the color sequence indicated to complete the pillow top.

To finish

Refer to directions for Pillow 1 (page 134) and finish in same way.

Soft as a Cloud

The very first quilt for a new baby should fit the bassinet. When the baby outgrows the bassinet, the quilt can be used in the carriage or stroller. It's easy to make in a weekend. The finished quilt is 24 × 32 inches.

MATERIALS

Note: Yardages are figured for fabric 45 inches wide.
¼ yard white solid fabric
¼ yard pink solid fabric
1 yard blue calico (includes backing)
1 yard batting
3¼ yards 2-inch-wide eyelet
3¼ yards 1-inch-wide eyelet
1 skein pink embroidery floss for tying
tracing paper
cardboard

CUTTING LIST

Note: All measurements include a ¼-inch seam allowance. Trace patterns A and B and transfer them to cardboard for templates (see page 13).

Cut the following:
from white solid:
  48 A
from pink solid:
  48 A
from blue calico:
  backing piece 24½ × 32½
  48 B

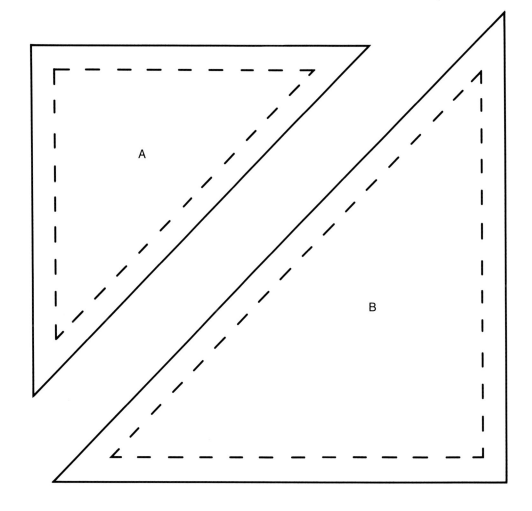

A

B

DIRECTIONS

To make blocks

1. Refer to Figure 1. With right sides facing, join a white A piece to a pink A piece along one short edge to make a larger triangle as shown.

2. Open seams and press. Make 48 pieced triangles in this way.

3. Refer to Figure 2. With right sides facing, stitch a pieced triangle to a blue calico B piece along the diagonal to make a square.

4. Open seams and press. Make 48 squares in this way.

5. Refer to Figure 3. With right sides facing, stitch 4 of these squares together to make a block as shown.

6. Open seams and press. Make 12 blocks in this way.

To make a row

1. Refer to Figure 4. With right sides facing, stitch 2 blocks together along the side edges.

A
A

Figure 1

B

Figure 2

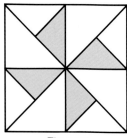

Figure 3

138

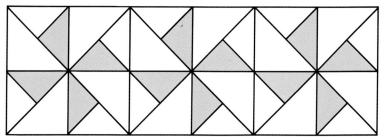

Figure 4

2. Continue with another block to make a row of 3 blocks as shown.

3. Open seams and press. Make 4 rows in this way.

To join rows

1. Refer to Figure 5. With right sides facing, stitch the bottom edge of a row to the top edge of another row.

2. Open seams and press.

3. Continue to join all 4 rows in this way to make the quilt top.

To add eyelet trim

1. With raw edges matching, pin the 1-inch-wide eyelet to the front of the 2-inch-wide eyelet and stitch across the raw edge to join.

2. With right sides facing and raw edges aligned, pin the raw edge of the eyelet to the quilt top all around. Overlap the ends where they meet.

3. Stitch all around.

To finish

1. With right sides facing, pin the backing and the quilt top together with the eyelet between.

2. Center this over the quilt batting and pin all 3 layers together. There will be extra batting all around.

3. Trim the excess batting to same size as the fabric.

4. Stitch around 4 corners and 3 sides, leaving the bottom edge open for turning. Turn right side out.

5. Turn the raw edges of the opening to the inside ¼ inch and press.

6. Slip-stitch the open edge closed.

7. Use the embroidery floss to tie the center of each block in the following way: Cut a length of floss 12 inches but do not make a knot on the end. Insert the needle through the top of the quilt in the center of the first block, then up again in the same spot. Make a knot, then a bow, and cut the ends of the floss. You will need approximately 6 inches for each bow.

Figure 5

Jody's Star Bright

Star patterns have always been popular with quiltmakers. For this quilt, Maggie Detmer set each pastel star on a background of black and surrounded each block with red. Then she bordered the entire quilt with purple fabric. This quilt, which measures 70 × 94 inches, was made for her oldest son, Jody.

MATERIALS

Note: Yardages are figured for fabric 45 inches wide.

¼ yard each of pale blue, pink, yellow, gray, turquoise, brown, ecru, and purple fabrics for the stars

1½ yards black solid fabric

2 yards dark red solid fabric

2 yards deep purple solid fabric

5½ yards backing fabric (navy blue or black)

quilt batting 72 × 96 inches

tracing paper

cardboard

quilt marking pen

CUTTING LIST

Note: All measurements include a ¼-inch seam allowance.

Trace patterns A, B, and C and transfer them to cardboard for templates (see page 13).

Cut the following:

(There are 8 B pieces and 1 C piece in each block. Cut the same color B and C pieces for each block.)

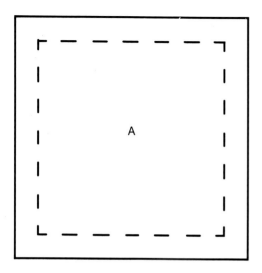

from star fabrics:
    240 B
     30 C
from black solid:
    120 A
    240 B
from red solid:
    2 strips, each $3\frac{1}{2} \times 69\frac{1}{2}$ inches (side borders)
    7 strips, each $3\frac{1}{2} \times 52\frac{1}{2}$ inches (top and bottom borders/
      lattice strips)
    24 strips, each $3\frac{1}{2} \times 8\frac{1}{2}$ inches (lattice strips)
from deep purple solid:
    2 strips, each $12\frac{1}{2} \times 69\frac{1}{2}$ inches (top and bottom borders)
    2 strips, each $6 \times 69\frac{1}{2}$ inches (side borders)

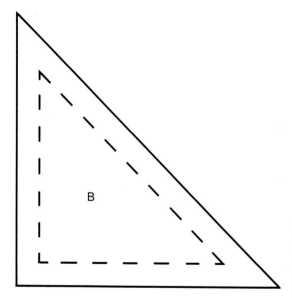

DIRECTIONS

To make a block

1. Refer to Figure 1. With right sides facing, join a star fabric B piece to a black B piece along the diagonal to make a square.
2. Press seams to the dark side. Make 8 of these squares using the same color.
3. Refer to Figure 2. With right sides facing, join 2 of these squares along the black edge to make a rectangle as shown.
4. Press seams to one side. Make 4 of these rectangles.
5. Refer to Figure 3 and, with right sides facing, join an A piece to a pieced rectangle along one side edge, followed by another A piece to make a row.
6. Next, join a pieced rectangle to a C square, followed by another pieced rectangle as shown. Press seams to one side.
7. Repeat Step 5.
8. Refer to Figure 4. With right sides facing and seams aligned, join all 3 sections as shown. Press seams to one side to complete the block. Make 30 blocks in this way.

To make a row

Refer to Figure 5.
1. With right sides facing, join a 3½ × 8½-inch red lattice strip to the right side edge of a block. Press seams to one side.
2. With right sides facing, join another block to the long edge of the lattice strip. Press seams to one side.
3. Continue to join blocks with the short red lattice strips to make a row of 5 blocks and 4 lattice strips.
4. Press seams to one side. Make 6 rows in this way.

To join rows

Refer to Figure 6.
1. With right sides facing, join a 3½ × 52½-inch red lattice strip to the top edge of the first row. Press seams to one side.

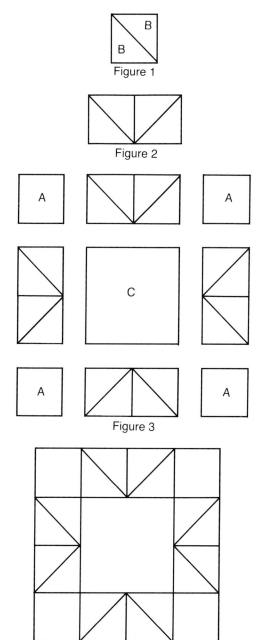

Figure 1

Figure 2

Figure 3

Figure 4

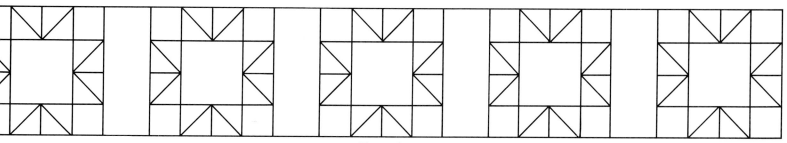

Figure 5

Figure 6

2. Next, join another red lattice strip to the bottom edge of the first row in the same way.
3. With right sides facing, join the bottom edge of that lattice strip to the top edge of Row 2. Press seams to one side.
4. Continue to join all 6 rows with the long red lattice strips, ending with a lattice strip across the bottom edge of the last row. Press seams to one side.
5. With right sides facing, stitch one of the remaining 2 red strips (3½ × 69½ inches) to each side edge of the quilt top.
6. Press seams to one side.

To add borders

1. Refer to Figure 6. With right sides facing, join a 6 × 69½-inch deep purple border strip to one side edge of the quilt top. Press seams to one side.
2. Repeat on the opposite side edge of the quilt.
3. Next, join the 12½ × 69½-inch remaining deep purple border strips to the top and bottom edges of the quilt top.
4. Press seams to one side.

To prepare the backing

1. Cut the backing fabric in half crosswise to make two pieces, each 45 × 99 inches.
2. With right sides facing, stitch the 2 pieces together along one long edge to make a piece 89½ × 99 inches.
3. Press seams to one side.

To prepare quilting

1. (See page 13 for transferring quilting patterns). Trace Quilting Patterns 1 and 2.
2. Start in the center of the top purple border and transfer Pattern 1. Turn Pattern 1 over and transfer again to create a circle. Add another circle ¾-inches larger all around. Continue to transfer Pattern 1 on each side of the center working toward each outer edge.
3. Repeat on the bottom purple border.
4. Next, transfer Pattern 2 to each side purple border.
5. Place a yardstick on the diagonal across one corner of the red border and measure and mark evenly spaced lines across the quilt top, stopping short of the purple borders.

To quilt

1. With wrong sides facing and the batting between, pin backing, batting, and quilt top together.
2. Beginning at the center and working outward in a sunburst pattern, take long, loose basting stitches through all 3 layers, stopping short of the seam allowance around the outside edges.
3. Using small running stitches, quilt on all premarked lines, stopping short of the seam allowance around the edges.

To finish

1. When all quilting is complete, remove the basting stitches.
2. Trim the batting ¼ inch smaller than the quilt top all around.
3. Trim the backing so it's 1 inch larger than the quilt top all around.
4. Turn the raw edges of the backing fabric forward ¼ inch and press.
5. Fold the remaining fabric forward over the top of the quilt to create a ½-inch border all around. Press and pin.
6. Slip-stitch the border to the quilt top to finish.

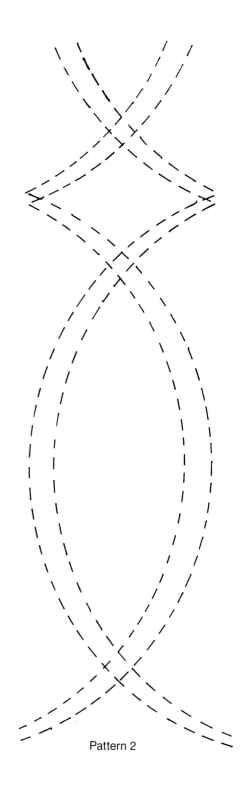

Pattern 2

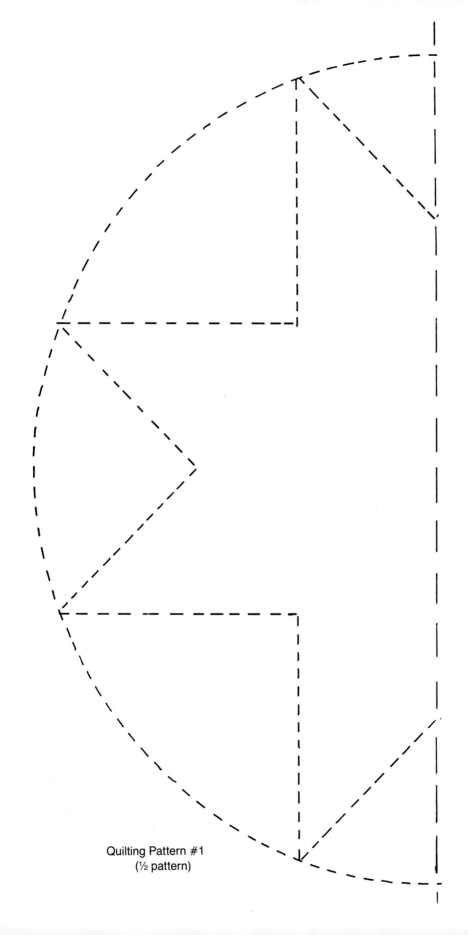

Quilting Pattern #1
(½ pattern)

Max's Log Cabin

The Log Cabin design is as popular today as it was when it was originally made by Early American quilters. There are so many variations that are possible. Some quilters like to use light and dark prints of different colors, others like to use varying shades of the same colors ranging from light to dark. This quilt gets its vitality from the use of lots of different colors in light, medium, and dark shades.

Maggie Detmer has been sharing her quilts with us for a long time. Her quilts are distinguished by her creative use of colors. All her quilts have an Amish feeling and she used the scraps from her Amish quilts to make this one for her youngest son, Max. When we borrowed it to take the photograph he was most unhappy to be without his quilt, even for one day. The finished quilt is 61 × 61 inches.

MATERIALS

Note: Yardages are figured for fabric 45 inches wide.

¼ yard each of 6 different light-color solid fabrics as follows:
  yellow, pale blue, peach, pink, pale green, pale purple

¼ yard each of 6 different medium-color solid fabrics as follows:
  purple, olive, rose, blue, tangerine, plum

¼ yard light green solid fabric (corners of borders)

1 yard black solid fabric

3¾ yards blue solid fabric (backing and borders)

2 yards quilt batting

tracing paper

cardboard

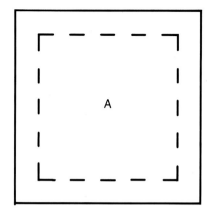

CUTTING LIST

Note: All measurements include a ¼-inch seam allowance.

Trace patterns A, B, C, and D and transfer them to cardboard for templates (see page 13).

Cut the following:

from light colors:
  (Use 1 A piece and 1 C piece of a matching color in each block.)
  64 A
  64 C

from medium colors:
  (Use 1 B piece and 1 D piece of matching color in each block.)
  64 B
  64 D

from black solid:
  (Use 1 A piece, 1 B piece, and 1 C piece in each block.)
  64 A
  64 B
  64 C

from light green solid:
  4 squares, each 6½ × 6½ inches

from blue solid:
  (Cut backing pieces first.)
  2 pieces, each 32 × 64 inches (backing)
  4 strips, each 6½ × 48½ inches (borders)

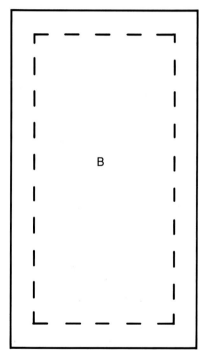

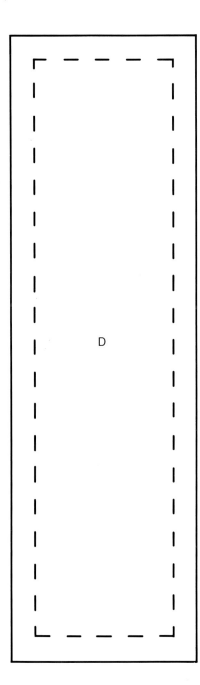

D

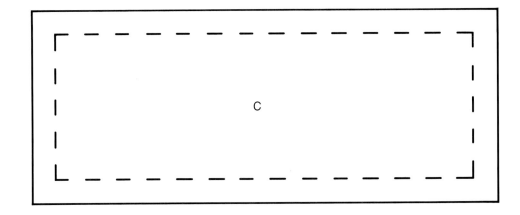

C

DIRECTIONS
To make a block

1. Refer to Figure 1. With right sides facing, stitch a black A piece to a light A piece to make a rectangle. Press seams to the dark side.

2. Refer to Figure 2 and stitch a medium B piece to the bottom edge of this rectangle to make a square. Press seams to the dark side.

3. Refer to Figure 3. With right sides facing, stitch a black B piece to the left side edge of this square. Press seams to the dark side.

4. Refer to Figure 4. With right sides facing, stitch a black C piece to the top edge of the square. Press seams to the dark side.

5. Refer to Figure 5. With right sides facing, stitch a light C piece to the right side edge of this square. Press seams to one side.

6. Refer to Figure 6 and stitch a medium D piece to the bottom edge of the square to complete the block. Press seams to one side.

7. Make 64 blocks in this way.

Figure 1

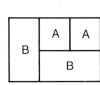

Figure 2

Figure 3

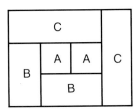

Figure 4

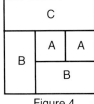

Figure 5

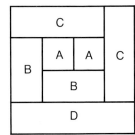

Figure 6

To join blocks

Refer to Figure 7.
1. Using 8 blocks for each of the 8 rows, arrange the blocks
so the black corners of each are in position as shown.
2. With right sides facing and seams aligned, join all 8
blocks in each of the 8 rows.
3. Press seams to one side.

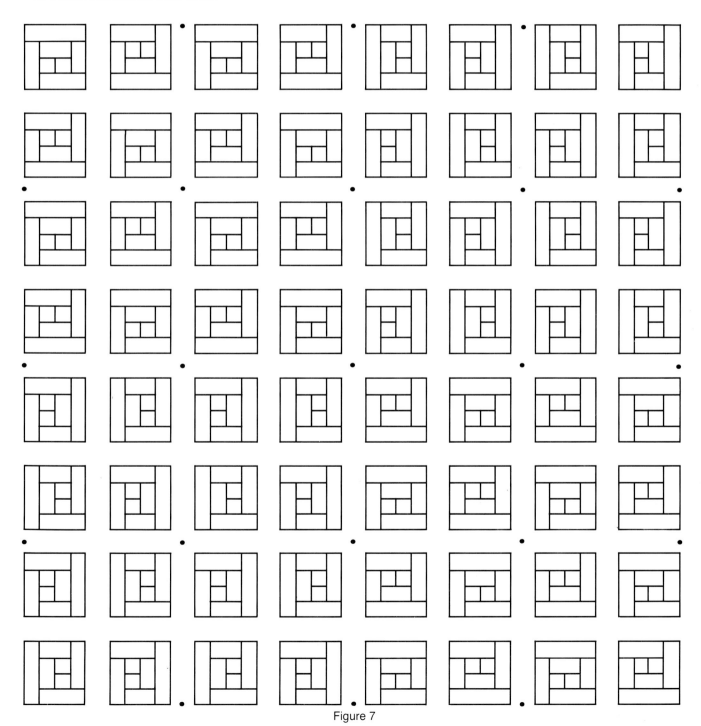

Figure 7

Figure 8

To join rows

1. With right sides facing and seams aligned, stitch the bottom edge of the first row to the top edge of the second row.
2. Press seams to one side.
3. Next, stitch the bottom edge of Row 2 to the top edge of Row 3.
4. Continue in this way to join all 8 rows to make the quilt top.
5. Press seams to one side.

To join borders

Refer to Figure 8.
1. With right sides facing, join a blue border strip to each side of the quilt top.
2. Press seams to one side.
3. With right sides facing, join a light green square to each

short end of the remaining 2 blue border strips to make longer strips.

4. Next, with right sides facing, stitch 1 of these longer pieced strips to the top edge of the quilt top. Stitch the remaining strip to the bottom edge of the quilt top in the same way.

5. Press seams to one side.

To prepare backing

1. With right sides facing, join the 2 backing pieces along the long edge.

2. Open seams and press.

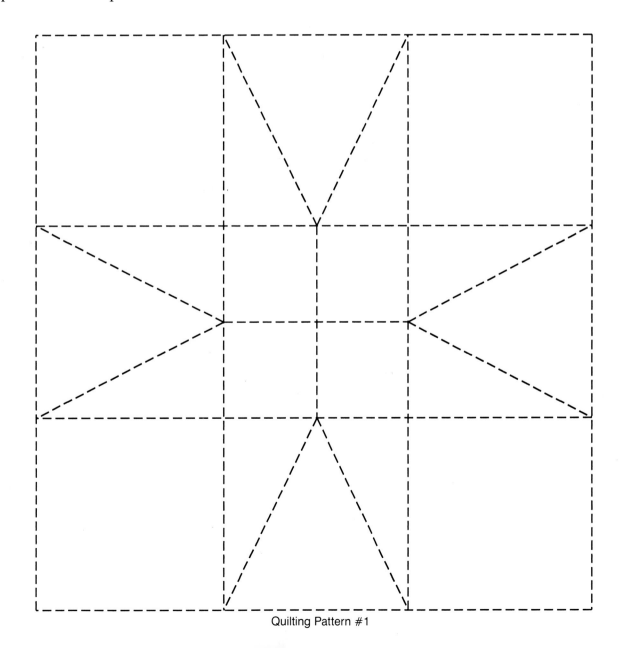

Quilting Pattern #1

153

Quilting Pattern #2

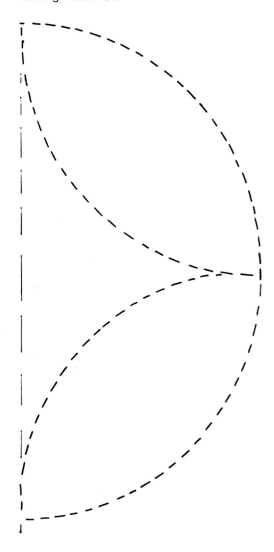

Preparing to quilt

1. See page 13 for instructions for transferring quilting patterns. Trace Quilting Patterns 1 and 2.
2. Transfer Pattern 1 to each of the light green squares of the border.
3. Transfer Pattern 2 to the middle of a blue border, then repeat, reversing alternate motifs and working toward the ends. Repeat on the other borders.
4. The body of the quilt is quilted with overlapping sets of concentric circles. The center of the quilt is the center of the first set of concentric circles. The centers of the other sets are the intersections of alternate quilt blocks (the dots between the blocks on Figure 7). Mark these centers with a quilt marker or pin.
5. Make a compass from a push pin, quilt marker and a length of string. Place the push-pin end at each of the marked center points and, adjusting the length of the string as necessary, mark a set of concentric circles at each: Begin at the center of the quilt and refer to the photographs as you do this.

To quilt

1. With wrong sides facing and the batting between, pin the backing, batting, and quilt top together.
2. Beginning at the center and working outward in a sunburst pattern, baste all 3 layers together with long, loose stitches.
3. Using small, running stitches, quilt on all premarked quilting lines, stopping short of the ¼-inch seam allowance all around.

To finish

1. When all quilting is complete, remove the basting stitches.
2. Trim the batting to same size as the quilt top.
3. Trim the backing so there is 1 inch extra all around the quilt top.
4. Turn the raw edge of the backing fabric forward ¼ inch and press. Then turn the remaining backing fabric forward onto the top of the quilt to create a ½-inch border all around. Press and pin to the quilt.
5. Slip-stitch the blue border to the quilt top all around.

Lover's Knot

This wall hanging, with its romantic name, is perfect to make for giving as a wedding gift. The finished size is 54 inches square. It would look quite nice hanging over a bed. If possible, use fabric that matches the room in which it will hang.

MATERIALS
Note: Yardages are figured for fabric 45 inches wide.
1½ yards dark floral print (A)
1½ yards white print (B)
1½ yards light floral print (C)
3½ yards cranberry print (D) (includes backing)
54 × 54 inch quilt batting
1 skein embroidery floss to match a color in the quilt for
   tying

CUTTING LIST
Note: All measurements include a ¼-inch seam allowance.

Cut the following:
from dark floral print (A):
   (Cut these pieces vertically first.)
   2 strips, each 1½ × 53½ inches (side borders)
   2 strips, each 1½ × 51½ inches (top and bottom borders)
   4 strips, each 2½ × 39½ inches
   16 squares, each 2½ × 2½ inches
from white print (B):
   (Cut these pieces vertically first.)

2 strips, each 1½ × 51½ inches (side borders)
2 strips, each 1½ × 49½ inches (top and bottom borders)
6 squares, each 8⅞ × 8⅞ inches (Cut each square along
  the diagonal into 2 triangles, for a total of 12 triangles)
1 square, 9¼ × 9¼ inches (Cut along the diagonal in both
  directions to make 4 triangles.)
5 strips, each 2½ × 39 inches
from light floral print (C):
  (Cut these pieces vertically first.)
  2 strips, each 2½ × 49½ inches (side borders)
  2 strips, each 2½ × 45½ inches (top and bottom borders)
  9 strips, each 2½ × 35 inches
from cranberry print (D):
  (Cut backing pieces vertically first.)
  2 pieces, each 30 × 58 inches (backing)
  8 strips, each 2½ × 30 inches
  9 squares, each 2½ × 2½ inches

DIRECTIONS
To make Block 1
1. Refer to Figure 1. With right sides facing, join a white (B) strip to the bottom edge of a dark floral (A) square as shown. Cut off the excess B fabric as shown.
2. Refer to Figure 2 and stitch the white (B) strip to the right side edge of the A/B piece. Cut off the excess B fabric.
3. Press seams to one side.
4. Refer to Figure 3. With right sides facing, join a light floral (C) strip to the bottom edge of the square as shown. Cut off the excess C fabric.
5. Refer to Figure 4. Continuing with the light floral (C) strip, stitch down the right side of the block. Cut off the excess C fabric.
6. Press seams to one side.
7. Refer to Figure 5. With right sides facing, stitch a cranberry (D) strip across the bottom edge of the block. Cut off the excess D fabric.
8. Refer to Figure 6. Continuing with the cranberry (D) strip, stitch down the right side of the block. Cut off the remainder of the D strip.
9. Press seams to one side to complete Block 1. Make 16 blocks in this way.

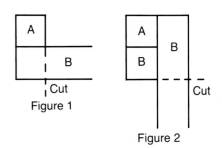

Figure 1

Figure 2

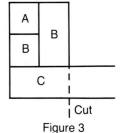

Figure 3

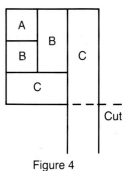

Figure 4

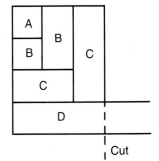

Figure 5

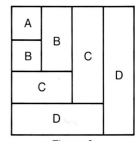

Figure 6

Block 1

157

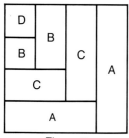

Figure 7
Block 2

To make Block 2

Refer to Figure 7.

1. Beginning with a cranberry (D) square in step 1 and ending with a dark floral (A) strip for steps 7 and 8, follow Block 1 steps 1–9 to make Block 2.

2. Press seams to one side to complete Block 2. Make 9 blocks in this way.

To join blocks

Refer to Figure 8 for placement and directions of blocks. *Note:* Blocks are set on the diagonal.

1. With right sides facing, join the long diagonal edge of a small white triangle to the top edge of Block 1.

2. Next, join the short side edge of a large white triangle to each side of this block.

3. Press seams to one side.

4. With right sides facing, join the short side of another large white triangle to the left side of another Block 1. Then, stitch the right side of that Block 1 to the left side edge of a Block 2. Continue with another Block 1 followed by another large white triangle to complete Row 2.

5. Press seams to one side.

6. Refer to Figure 8. Continue to join blocks and triangles to make all 7 rows as shown.

7. Press seams to one side.

To join rows

1. With right sides facing and seams aligned, join the bottom edge of Row 1 to the top edge of Row 2.

2. Next, join the bottom edge of Row 2 to the top edge of Row 3.

3. Continue to join all 7 rows in this way.

4. Press seams to one side.

To join borders

Refer to Figure 9.

1. With right sides facing, join the shorter light floral (C) border strips to the top and bottom edges of the quilt top.

2. Next, stitch the 2 remaining light floral (C) border strips to the sides of the quilt top.

3. Press seams to one side.

4. With right sides facing, join the shorter white (B) border strips to the top and bottom edges of the quilt top.

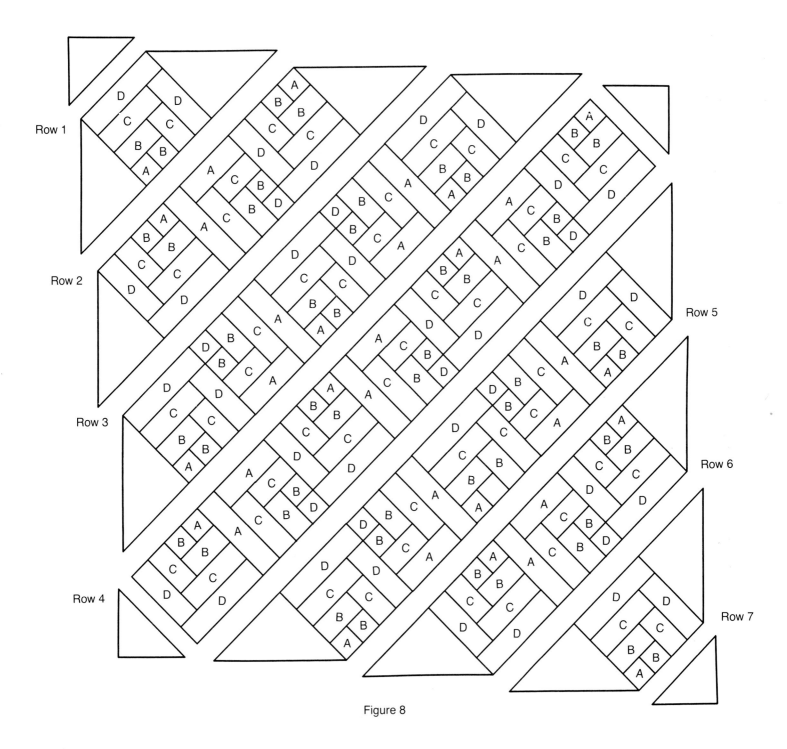

Figure 8

159

Figure 9

5. Next, join the 2 remaining white (B) border strips to the sides of the quilt top.

6. Press seams to one side.

7. With right sides facing, join the shorter dark floral (A) border strips to the top and bottom edges of the quilt top.

8. Then, join the 2 remaining dark floral (A) border strips to the side edges of the quilt top.

9. Press seams to one side.

To make backing and prepare quilt for tying

1. With right sides facing, stitch the 2 cranberry backing pieces together along the long edge.

2. Press seams to one side.

3. With wrong sides facing and the batting between (there will be extra batting and fabric all around the quilt top), pin backing, batting, and top together.

4. Beginning at the center and working outward in a sunburst pattern, baste the 3 layers together with long loose stitches.

5. Using embroidery floss, tie the quilt through all 3 layers at each corner of each block. (See page 16 for instructions on tying a quilt).

To finish

1. When all tying is complete, remove the pins and the basting stitches.

2. Trim batting to same size as quilt top all around.

3. Trim backing so it's 1 inch larger than the quilt top all around.

4. Turn the raw edges of the backing to the inside ¼ inch on each side and press.

5. Next, turn each edge of the backing over onto the quilt top to create a ½-inch border of cranberry all around. Press and pin to the quilt top.

6. Slip-stitch the border to the quilt top or machine-stitch all around.

Flying South

This is a particularly pretty rendition of a traditional pattern made up of triangles. You will employ the quick-and-easy triangle method to make up all the squares. This is a good way to use up remnants from other projects. While we used solid pastels with white, you can use printed light and dark fabrics as well.

The finished size of the quilt is 64 × 80 inches with 8 rows of 10 squares each and will fit a full or queen-size bed. To make a single-bed quilt measuring 48 × 72 inches, make 6 rows of 9 squares each. For a wall hanging that measures 48 × 48 inches, make 6 rows of 6 squares each.

MATERIALS

Note: Yardages are figured for fabric 45 inches wide.

¾ yards each of solid fabric in the following colors: yellow (A), green (B), rose (C), orange (D), pink (E), peach (J), and aqua (K)

½ yard each of solid fabric in the following colors: blue (F), lavender (G), ochre (H), and red (I)

3½ yards white solid fabric

4 yards backing fabric

quilt batting 64 × 80 inches

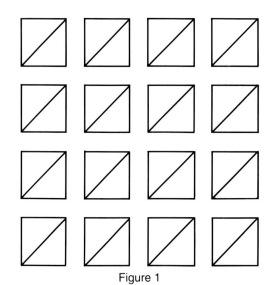

Figure 1

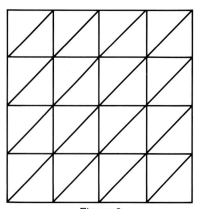

Figure 2

CUTTING LIST

Note: All measurements include a ¼ inch seam allowance.

Cut the following:

from white solid:
   4 squares, each 21 × 21 inches
   7 squares, each 24 × 24 inches
from A, B, C, D, E, J, and K:
   1 square from each, 24 × 24 inches
from F, G, H, and I:
   1 square from each, 21 × 21 inches

Quick-and-easy triangle method

1. Refer to page 16 for the quick-and-easy triangle techniques. On the wrong side of each piece of 21 × 21-inch white fabric, measure and mark 7 rows of 7 squares, each 2⅞ × 2⅞ inches.
2. With right sides facing, pin each marked piece of white fabric to a corresponding piece of F, G, H, and I fabrics.
3. Make 98 squares (2 extra) of each color.
4. On the wrong side of each piece of 24 × 24-inch white fabric, measure and mark 8 rows of 8 squares, each 2⅞ × 2⅞ inches.
5. With right sides facing, pin each marked white piece of fabric to a corresponding piece of A, B, C, D, and E fabrics.
6. Make 128 squares (no extra) of each color.

To make a block

1. Refer to Figure 1. With right sides facing, join an A-and-white square to another A-and-white square along the right side edge.
2. Press seams to one side.
3. Continue to join 2 more A-and-white squares in this way to complete Row 1. Make 4 rows in this way.
4. Refer to Figure 2. With right sides facing and seams aligned, join the bottom edge of Row 1 to the top edge of Row 2. Press seams to one side.
5. Continue to join Rows 3 and 4 in the same way to complete the block. Make 8 blocks in this way.
6. Repeat steps 1–5 to make 8 blocks each of B, C, D, E, J, and K and 6 blocks each of the F, G, H, and I.

To make rows

Refer to Figure 3.

1. With right sides facing and seams aligned, join an A block to a B block along the right side edge. Press seams to one side.

2. With right sides facing, join a C block, followed by a D block, then an E block, followed by an A block, then a G block, and end with a C block to complete Row 1.

3. Press all seams to one side.

4. Refer to Figure 2 and make Rows 2 through 10 in the same way.

Row 1	A	B	C	D	E	A	G	C
Row 2	E	F	H	K	J	I	H	B
Row 3	K	C	G	A	F	B	J	E
Row 4	D	K	E	I	J	G	K	D
Row 5	B	C	D	A	F	H	J	I
Row 6	C	G	A	E	D	C	B	A
Row 7	B	H	I	J	K	H	F	E
Row 8	E	J	B	F	A	G	C	K
Row 9	D	K	G	J	I	E	K	D
Row 10	I	J	H	F	A	D	C	B

Key
A Yellow
B Green
C Rose
D Orange
E Pink
F Blue
G Lavender
H Ochre
I Red
J Peach
K Aqua

Figure 3

To join rows

1. With right sides facing and seams aligned, join the bottom edge of Row 1 and the top edge of Row 2.
2. Press seams to one side.
3. Continue to join all 10 rows in this way to complete the quilt top.

To prepare backing

1. Cut the backing fabric in half crosswise. Cut one piece in half lengthwise.
2. With right sides facing, join the 2 narrow pieces along each side edge of the larger piece to make a piece 72 × 88½ inches.
3. Press seams to one side.

To quilt

1. With wrong sides facing, center the quilt top and the batting on the backing fabric and pin all 3 layers together. There will be extra backing fabric all around.
2. Beginning at the center and working outward in a sunburst pattern, take long, loose basting stitches through all layers, stopping short of the seam allowance around the outside edges.
3. Using small running stitches, quilt ¼ inch on each side of all seam lines, stopping short of the seam allowance around the quilt top.

To finish

1. When all quilting is complete, remove the basting stitches.
2. Trim the batting ¼ inch smaller than the quilt top all around.
3. Trim the backing to the same size as the quilt top.
4. Turn the raw edges of the backing forward ¼ inch and press.
5. Turn the raw edges of the quilt top under ¼ inch and press.
6. Pin edges together and machine-stitch all around to finish.

Index

All of us at Meredith® Press are dedicated to offering you quality craft books. We welcome your comments and suggestions. Please address your correspondence to: Customer Service, Meredith Press, Meredith Corporation, 150 East 52nd Street, New York, NY 10022 or call 1-800-678-2665